Germany's
-SECRET WEAPONS-
IN WORLD WAR II

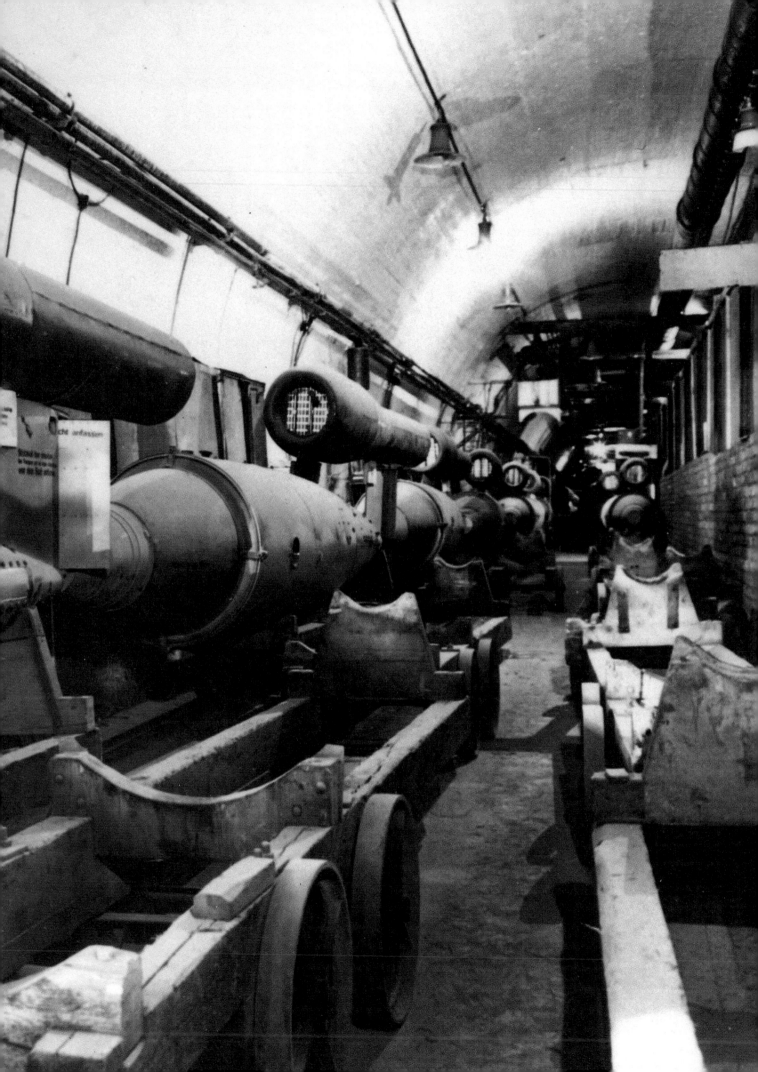

Germany's
—SECRET WEAPONS—
IN WORLD WAR II

Roger Ford

MBI Publishing Company

This edition first published in 2000 by
MBI Publishing Company,
729 Prospect Avenue, PO Box 1, Osceola, WI 54020-0001 USA

MBI Publishing Company books are also available at discounts in bulk quantity
for industrial or sales-promotional use. For details write to Special Sales Manager
at Motorbooks International Wholesalers & Distributors, 729 Prospect Avenue,
PO Box 1, Osceola, WI 54020-0001 USA

Library of Congress Cataloging-in-Publication Data Available

ISBN 0-7603-0847-0

Editorial and design: Amber Books Ltd
Bradley's Close, 74-77 White Lion Street,
London N1 9PF

Editor: Chris Marshall
Design: Brian Rust

Printed in The Slovak Republic

Picture credits: Hugh W. Cowin: 6, 12, 15(t), 21(b), 36, 43, 46, 54, 56, 59, 62(both), 90, 95(b), 97, 98(t), 99, 100, 107.
Robert Hunt Library: 20, 27, 29(t), 60, 64, 70, 74, 76, 79, 93, 106, 108, 113, 119, 126(both). Salamander Picture
Library: 2, 96, 102, 105. TRH Pictures: 7, 8(US National Archives), 14, 18-19(US National Archives), 21(t)(IWM), 22,
23(t), 24(US National Archives), 26(b)(US National Archives), 28(IWM), 29(b), 31(US National Archives), 32(US
National Archives), 34(US National Archives), 39(US National Archives), 42(US National Archives), 44(US National
Archives), 49, 52, 57(US National Archives), 63, 65, 66(IWM), 67, 69(t), 72, 73(IWM), 75(US National Archives),
78(US National Archives), 82(US National Archives), 83(Associated Press), 84(National Air and Space Museum),
86(US National Archives), 89(US National Archives), 112(US National Archives), 114, 115, 116, 120, 123(Tank
Museum), 125(US National Archives), 128(IWM), 130(US National Archives), 132(b)(US National Archives), 134(US
National Archives), 135(t), 135(b)(IWM), 136(IWM), 137(US National Archives), 138(US National Archives), 140(US
National Archives), 141(US National Archives).

All Illustrations Aerospace Publishing except: John Bachelor: 124. Pilot Press Limited: 16-17. Wieslaw Baczkowski:
38, 40, 50-51.

Page 2: Fieseler Fi 103s – V1s – line the corridor of an underground factory.

Contents

Introduction

Before we begin to examine the large and diverse array of secret weapons produced in Germany before and during World War II, we should perhaps define what is meant by the term 'secret'. Most weapons are developed in secret – or at least, under conditions of stringent security – whether in times of peace or war, if only because, as the old adage has it, forewarned is forearmed. In Germany's case, there was an added imperative: the Versailles Treaty which, at the end of World War I, forbade her to develop (and even to possess) certain categories of weapons, such as aircraft and tanks. Development programmes for these weapons had to be carried out in absolute secrecy, since the ultimate risk (though probably a small one by the time these development programmes were under way) was the occupation of Germany by the victorious Allies. In many cases, up until the moment that Hitler signalled his intention to revoke the Treaty unilaterally, the projects were actually based outside Germany: in Holland, the Soviet Union, Sweden and in particular Switzerland.

In the strict sense, then, when we address the topic of German secret weapons of World War II, we are faced with an enormous task. But the term 'secret weapons' has a more precise meaning in general use: it implies something which goes beyond the development of a piece of more or less mundane equipment in conditions of secrecy. It implies a genuinely new concept, something truly out of the ordinary, which simply could not work without a new understanding of physical science or chemistry; a new mastery of technology; or some great leap of creative, imaginative invention. In the place and at the time in question, there was certainly no lack of those.

WUNDERWAFFEN

Perhaps the alternative term frequently used in Germany at the time – *Wunderwaffen* – comes closer to defining the true nature of these secret devices, for they were often truly things of wonder, being either completely new and hitherto undreamed-of outside a small select group, or achieving previously unthinkable levels of performance thanks to breakthrough innovations in science and technology. Some of them, it is true, were 'ideas whose time had come', in that the basic principle was understood, but had not yet been successfully applied, and in these cases, teams of scientists and engineers in America, Britain and Germany (and sometimes elsewhere: there were several significant advances made by Italy) were engaged in a headlong race to get the first reliable working version onto the battlefield. The development of the jet aircraft and of radar, not to mention the development of nuclear fission, stand out amongst those. But in other areas, particularly in rocketry and the invention and perfection of the all-important guidance systems, Germany stood head and shoulders above the rest.

Left: The Junkers Ju 287, with its forward-swept wings, was just one of a number of futuristic designs developed by German scientists and engineers in World War II.

Above: A borderline secret weapon: the 'Goliath' was an explosives-filled wire-guided tank and a typically innovative approach to dealing with bunkers and armour.

Her scientists made an enormous and outstanding contribution, not just to the German war effort, but to modern civilisation. However, there were areas where German science and technology were deficient, most importantly – arguably – in the field of electronic computing machines, which were not weapons themselves but something without which the bounds of technological development would soon be reached. However, all too often these deficiencies arose as a result of demand chasing insufficient resource, and time simply ran out for the scientists of the Third Reich before a satisfactory result could be produced.

TOO LITTLE, TOO LATE

Time and again in the course of this work we will come upon development programmes which were either cancelled before they came to fruition or which were still in progress at the war's end. Many of them, of course, did not get under way until 1944, when the spectre of defeat was already looming large in Berlin and many essential items were in increasingly short supply. We can only speculate upon the possible outcome of an earlier start on the course of the conflict. Others were cancelled simply because they did not appear to offer the likelihood of spectacular results, and in those cases we can, all too often, detect the hand of Adolf Hitler. In general, we can note what can only be described as a wrong-headed insistence on his part that big (and powerful) was always beautiful (and irresistible). This major flaw led him to push for the development of weapons such as the fearsome – but only marginally effective and very expensive – PzKpfw VI Tiger and King Tiger tanks, which would have been far better consigned to the wastebin from

the very outset, and the resources squandered upon producing them – and then keeping them in service – redirected into more appropriate channels such as the more practical PzKpfw V Panther.

In a very real sense, Hitler himself motivated and ran the German secret weapons programme. There seems to be a direct and very tangible link between this programme and his psyche, and we are perhaps left wondering whether the *Wunderwaffen* would have existed without him. On balance, it seems certain that they would have done, given the creative imagination of so many German scientists and the readiness of many of her military men to accept innovation, but it is equally certain that without Hitler's insistence, many weapons systems which made a very real impact upon the course of the war would either not have been developed at all, or would, at best, have been less prominent.

Nonetheless, without the genius of many German scientists and the brilliance of German technologists and engineers, the entire programme would have been stillborn. Many of the weapons produced for the first time in Germany and employed in World War II went on to become accepted and very important parts of the broader armoury, and several have made an enormous impact on life as a whole outside the military arena. The more spectacular failures have a certain grandeur, despite their shortcomings, and even the outright myths – and there were many, some remarkably persistent – frequently had an underpinning of fact.

CHAPTER ONE

Jet Aircraft

Thrust-powered flight was an early alternative to the airscrew propeller – in 1928, only a quarter century after the Wright brothers first took to the air, Fritz Stammer flew in a rocket-powered glider. By the time a further decade had gone by, both rocket- and jet-powered aircraft had become a reality, and a central plank in Germany's attempts to win control in the air.

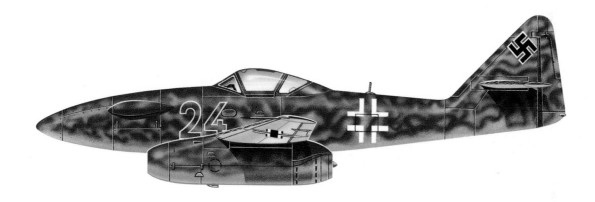

The German Air Force, the Luftwaffe, was held in high esteem in National Socialist Party (henceforth, Nazi) circles, and it perhaps enjoyed better access to the ultimate seat of power, namely Adolf Hitler, than the Army or the Navy. This was not just because it had at its head one of the Führer's closest associates, Hermann Göring, but also because for almost all of the war, it had sole charge of the front-line defence of Germany against the combined onslaughts of the British and American air forces, bombing by night and by day.

Certainly, when it came to the allocation of funds for research and development, the Luftwaffe was at the head of the line; as a result, more developments

Above: The stark shape of the Messerschmitt Me 262.

Left: The Heinkel He 162 made use of appropriate technology – in this case, plywood; its wing and tailplane assemblies were manufactured in furniture factories.

were made in the field of aeronautics in the Third Reich than in any other. That there was something approaching chaos in the way individual projects were initiated, approved and evaluated is a constant source of wonder, because in a country which prided itself on its logical, methodical approach to problem-solving, there was no logic or method in evidence! As one expert has commented, the relationship between the individual aircraft and engine manufacturers and also between them and the Luftwaffe and the *Reichsluftfahrtministerium* (RLM – the German Air Ministry) looked like tribal warfare.

Those projects which came to fruition were amongst the better-known wartime developments, and not just in Germany, but that only tells half, or far less than half, the story. The vast majority fell by the wayside, some due to lack of time; others, quite properly, because they were flawed; still others because they were simply too fanciful and apparently far-fetched. Most of the more interesting new aircraft developed during World War II in Germany were to be powered by either turbojet or rocket motors, in both of which German scientists and engineers excelled, but as we shall see, the jet engine programme in particular was to get off to a very slow start. Had the optimism of the jet pioneers been justified, we might well have seen a different outcome to the war, a prolongation, perhaps, into the autumn and winter of 1945, which might have resulted in the nuclear bombs used against Japan being dropped on German cities, too. When it was so evident that the jet aircraft was going to be so vitally important, it comes as something of a surprise to see that the timescale of its development was so extended. As a result, although Germany had a very clear lead in the field, she squandered it, thanks largely to poor overall control of the research and development programme.

THE HEINKEL He 178

The name Heinkel deserves to figure high in any list of notable achievements in aviation, for it was from Ernst Heinkel's design studio, and specifically from the drawing boards of twin brothers Siegfried and Walter Günter, that the first practical thrust-powered aircraft – the rocket-propelled He 176 and the turbojet-powered He 178 – were to come. Heinkel himself, with partner Hellmuth Hirth, had enjoyed considerable success with the Albatros aircraft, especially the B.1, during World War I. He struggled through the dark days of the 1920s and came to prominence again with a commercial aircraft, the Günter-designed He 70 and, using that as a stepping-stone, produced arguably the most effective bomber of its day, the He 111, which first flew in early 1935. Heinkel continued to develop successful piston-engined aircraft, but his

interest also turned to the emerging technology of rocketry. There had been thrust-powered flights – Fritz Stammer flew a solid-fuel rocket-powered glider for the first time on 11 June 1928 – but it took almost a further decade and the development of liquid-fuelled motors to make it a practical proposition, as we shall discover in Chapter Two when we come to examine rocket-propelled aircraft.

Rocket motors, while they could hardly be called 'tried and tested' by 1938, were simple in the extreme; far more complicated, but offering huge advantages in terms of fuel economy and controllability, was the revolutionary new turbojet powerplant on which Heinkel's engineer, Joachim Pabst von Ohain, and his assistant Max Hahn, were working in secret. Lured away from Göttingen University, where they had done their pioneering work, the pair produced a first demonstration prototype, the HeS 1, which ran only on hydrogen (and was only barely controllable) to produce about 250kg (550lb) of static thrust, in September 1937. By the time six more months had passed, they had made considerable progress, and had produced the petrol-fuelled HeS 3, which developed 500kg (1100lb) of thrust. This, they believed, was a practical – if only marginally – powerplant, and the next step was to produce an airframe in which to mount it.

The result of their efforts was the He 178, the world's first jet-propelled aircraft. It was a shoulder-wing monoplane with its cockpit well forward of the wing leading edge, where it sat above the ducting

Below: The Heinkel He 178, despite its shortcomings, was the first jet-powered aircraft to fly successfully, on 27 August 1939, 20 months before Britain's Gloster E.28/39.

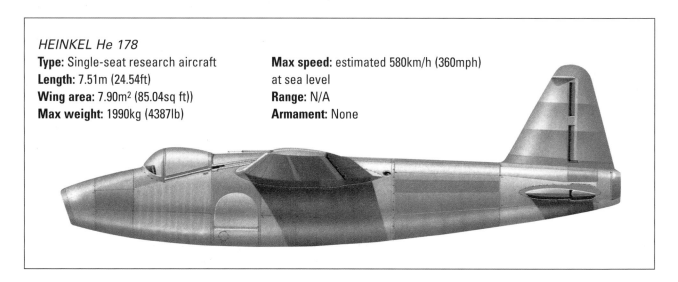

HEINKEL He 178
Type: Single-seat research aircraft
Length: 7.51m (24.54ft)
Wing area: 7.90m² (85.04sq ft)
Max weight: 1990kg (4387lb)
Max speed: estimated 580km/h (360mph) at sea level
Range: N/A
Armament: None

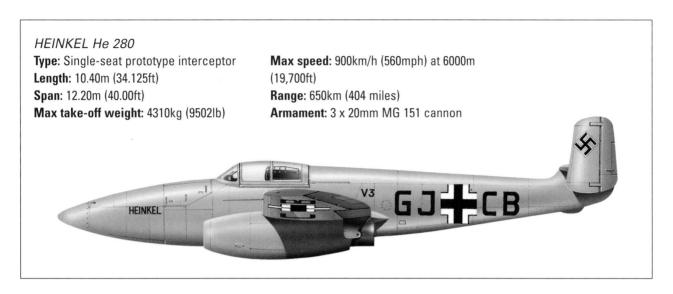

HEINKEL He 280
Type: Single-seat prototype interceptor
Length: 10.40m (34.125ft)
Span: 12.20m (40.00ft)
Max take-off weight: 4310kg (9502lb)

Max speed: 900km/h (560mph) at 6000m (19,700ft)
Range: 650km (404 miles)
Armament: 3 x 20mm MG 151 cannon

which brought air to the engine (which, along with its tailpipe, occupied most of the rest of the fuselage). It made its first true flight on 27 August 1939, having 'hopped' along the runway three days earlier. This pre-dated the maiden flight of the Gloster E.28/39, powered by Frank Whittle's engine, which had in its turn pre-dated Ohain's original effort, by over 20 months. The He 178 was demonstrated to the RLM on 1 November. Almost incredibly, there was virtually no official interest, and it (along with the He 176) was consigned to the Berlin Air Museum, where both were destroyed in an air raid in 1943.

THE HEINKEL He 280

Heinkel abandoned the He 178 largely because of technical problems associated with mounting the engine within the fuselage, but did not give up hope of developing a turbojet-powered fighter. New blood in the shape of Max Mueller arrived from Jumo to pep up the jet engine development programme. He worked on the the HeS 30, which became the 109-006. The 109- prefix was employed, somewhat confusingly, for both pulse-jet and turbojet engines and also for rocket motors; the three-figure designator following was allocated chronologically, and there is no logical distinction between one manufacturer and another. Thankfully, there were few enough engine types, so one soon became familiar with the rather impersonal system.

Simultaneous with Mueller's work was that of Pabst von Ohain who developed the HeS 3 as the HeS 8 (109-001). Both engines were to be tested in an all-new airframe, the He 280. This was a twin-engined aircraft, its powerplants slung beneath the low wings in nacelles and with a high tailplane with a fin and

Above: The second Heinkel jet, the He 280, was successful, but lost out in competition with the Messerschmitt Me 262. Just nine examples were built.

rudder at each tip. It made its first powered flight with von Ohain's engines on 2 April 1941, and was demonstrated to the Luftwaffe and RLM three days later.

Now the reaction was different. The immediate result was that Heinkel's engine division expanded in size with the addition of his old partner Hirth's company (which made piston engines and turbo-chargers amongst other things). Mueller and his team moved to the Hirth factory at Stuttgart, and von Ohain stayed at Rostock-Marienehe to work on a further development of his engine, the 109-011, which was projected to give 1300kg (2866lb) of static thrust. There was understandable rivalry between the two teams and both made considerable progress, but for some unaccountable reason, the RLM decided to order work on the 109-006 to be discontinued, even though it was already producing 900kg (1984lb) of thrust. Meanwhile, development of the 011 continued at Stuttgart, but even by the end of the war, it had never run except on a test bench and just 20 had been completed. Testing of the He 280 continued with both Jumo 004 and BMW 003 engines, but when it eventually came up against the Me 262, it fared badly. There are suggestions that the decision to adopt the Me 262 was at least partly politically motivated, since, as we have noted, the relationship between the various German planemakers themselves, and with the RLM and the Luftwaffe, was a political minefield. The nine prototypes constructed were later used for testing new wing and tail designs and Heinkel later worked on other jet aircraft designs, most of them centred on the

stillborn 011 engine, but none came to fruition until the submission which became the He 162 (qv) was accepted.

THE Me 262 'SCHWALBE'/'STURMVOGEL'

The best known of the aviation projects which actually came to fruition is the Messerschmitt Me 262, the aircraft chosen over the He 280. By modern standards, this was a fairly conventional all-metal fighter aircraft with gently swept low-set variable-chord wings, powered by twin Junkers Jumo 004B-1 turbojet engines. It became the first jet-powered aircraft to enter operational service, on 3 October 1944, and was thus a landmark in aviation history. We shall examine the development history of the Me 262 in more detail than other aircraft, both because it was so significant and because it will give us an insight into the methodology of aircraft development in the Third Reich, revealing that it was by no means a smooth process.

The Me 262 started life as a loosely defined project of the RLM, inaugurated in 1938, with Hans Mauch and Helmut Schlep working on the powerplant and Hans Antz on the airframe. Schlep, recently returned from college in the United States, had already convinced Junkers Motorenwerke (Jumo – the engine division of the forcibly nationalised planemaker) to start work on designs for axial-flow turbojets, and BMW, initially sub-contracted by Junkers, had also begun to develop a more sophisticated design of its own. In the meantime, Antz had interested Messerschmitt's chief of development, Robert Lusser, in examining the possibilities of producing an airframe to carry such a powerplant. Before the end of the year, the project had moved up a gear, and Messerschmitt

Above: A pre-production version of the Me 262 gets airborne with the help of solid-fuel rocket motors. Such 'RATO' (Rocket-Assisted Take-Off) units were widely used to assist heavily loaded aircraft into the air.

Below: In all, some 1430 Me 262s were to be produced in seven different variants. This bomber variant, the Me 262A-2a 'Sturmvogel', was operated by KG 51 out of Prague-Ruzyn in late 1944.

MESSERSCHMITT Me 262A-2a/U1
Type: Single-seat bomber
Length: 10.61m (34.79ft)
Span: 12.50m (41.01ft)
Max take-off weight: 6775kg (14,936lb)
Max speed: 870km/h (541mph) at 7000m (23,000ft)
Range: 845km (525 miles)
Armament: 2 x 30mm MK 108 cannon; 1000kg (2200lb) bombload

was instructed, somewhat baldly, to begin development work on a fighter aircraft which was to have an endurance of one hour at 850km/h (530mph). Responsibility was placed in the hands of Woldemar Voigt (of whom more later), who examined both single- and twin-engined arrangements before concluding that a single centrally mounted engine layout would present more problems than it would solve. His view was coloured by the performance of the He 178. Instead Voigt suggested a design with engines in each wing root, which crystallised into Project 1065 in Messerschmitt's Augsburg design office. Detailed design drawings were produced as early as 7 June 1939, and a wooden mock-up then made. On 3 March 1940 Messerschmitt was awarded a contract to produce three airframes, designated as the Me 262, for flight testing.

It was envisioned that the aircraft's power would come from two BMW P.3302 engines, delivery of which had been promised for the end of 1939, and their non-appearance was only the first of a long series of setbacks associated with the powerplant. In fact, the prototype BMW engine, now known as the 109-003, did not run until August 1940, and then it produced only 150kg (330lb) of static thrust instead of the 600kg (1320lb) promised. A year later it was still only producing 450kg (990lb), which was by no means enough to get the Me 262 into the air. It was to be mid-1943 before an 003 engine produced sufficient power to be viable, and a further year before production units became available, and in due course it was decided to reserve it for the Heinkel He 162 (see below). In addition, the BMW engine had proven too big to fit into the wing-root mount, and the design team had hurriedly modified the Me 262 to carry it in under-wing nacelles, though this, in turn, simplified main spar design. Some sources suggest that this factor, not the diameter of the BMW engines, underlay the decision to adopt nacelles rather than faired-in mountings, even at the expense of increased drag.

FIRST ALL-JET Me 262 FLIGHT

The Jumo 109-004 was always to have been a less sophisticated design, sacrificing ultimate potential for a 'fast track' into production. It, too, had its problems, however. The prototype ran in November 1940, but it was January 1942 before all the snags were ironed out, and its first flight, slung under a Messerschmitt Bf 110, took place on 15 March. The first pilot-production engines, 004As, which produced 840kg (1850lb) of static thrust, were rolled out in early summer, and were fitted to the Me 262 V3, which made

the first all-jet Me 262 flight on 18 July 1942 in the hands of Fritz Wendel. The aircraft had flown as early as 18 April 1941, but with a single 1200bhp Jumo 210G piston engine in its nose, and by that time an aircraft which was ultimately to be its closest competitor, the Heinkel He 280 (qv), had already flown on the power of two 500kg- (1100lb-) thrust HeS 8 turbojets. Orders for 15 Me 262s were placed, expanded to 60 by early October, by which time the second prototype had also flown, and the first Jumo 004B engines, with similar performance characteristics to the -As, were going into production.

PROPELLED BY AN ANGEL

On 22 April 1943, Adolf Galland, the operational head of the Luftwaffe, flew the aircraft himself (and returned to say it felt 'as if an angel were pushing me'), and was instrumental in convincing the RLM to switch most of Messerschmitt's production from the Bf 109 to the Me 262, the formal order for general production being issued on 5 June. On 26 June the production prototype, -V5, with a nosewheel undercarriage, took to the air. A blow fell on 17 August 1943: production of the Me 262 was just getting into

Below: The two-seater Me 262B-1 was normally employed as a night-fighter, but these aircraft lacked the distinctive 'toasting-fork' antenna on the nose, which, incidentally, slowed the night-fighter down.

full swing when the USAAF bombed the Messerschmitt factory at Regensburg, destroying much important tooling. The company's development programmes were transferred from Augsburg to Oberammergau as a result, with further attendant delays. By November, the future looked less bleak, with prototypes flying with pressurised cockpits and carrying armament (the as yet imperfect MG 108 30mm cannon) and with Junkers finally getting the 004B engine into series production, but then another quite different problem arose in the shape of direct interference from the Führer himself.

Senior Luftwaffe personnel, aware that they were losing the fight to limit the success of the RAF and USAAF bombing campaign, had begun to advocate that the production of bomber aircraft in the Third Reich should cease and that all efforts should concentrate on fighter types. Göring agreed, but Hitler recoiled at the very suggestion and would have none of it. Instead, he decided that the Me 262 would be perfect to carry a 500kg (1100lb) bombload to England to continue his pet campaign of harassment and nuisance raids, and he ordered the aircraft to be modified and developed for this purpose alone, even though it was hardly suitable and no adequate bombsight was available, nor was one ever produced.

It was May 1944 before Hitler agreed to allow production of the 'Schwalbe' ('Swallow') fighter version to continue, and then only in parallel with the

Above: This Me 262A, 'White 10' (the distinctive markings are largely obscured), was flown by Leutnant Kurt Bell of III/EJG 2 during the making of a Luftwaffe training film. Note the aircraft's pristine appearance.

'Sturmvogel' ('Storm Petrel') bomber, at the rate of one fighter to 20 bombers. Furthermore it was 4 November before he gave permission for it to go into unlimited production. By then, 13 pre-production Me 262A-0s had been completed, in addition to 12 development prototypes, and 60 more were scheduled to roll out during the following month. There was still much 'fine tuning' to be done, and versions of the aircraft, both bombers and fighters, were testing in a variety of forms, but more importantly, pilot training had begun. It was still to be five months before the Me 262 was ready to go to war, but essentially by mid-1944 the development emphasis had switched from Messerschmitt to the Luftwaffe, although the firm was still heavily involved, developing the two-seater trainer and night-fighter versions, as well as alternative forms for the stillborn *hochgeschwindigkeits* (HG – high speed) version.

In the final analysis, the Me 262 was simply too little, too late. The German jet scored its first confirmed combat victory in the hands of Leutnant Joachim Weber – his victim was a PR XVI Mosquito of No. 540 Squadron, RAF – on 8 August 1944, four days after the British Gloster 'Meteor' Mk 1 had made its combat debut (though admittedly, the latter's debut 'victory' had been over a pilotless V1 flying bomb). That bare statistic is a telling indictment, for the British had not flown their prototype jet aircraft, the E.28/39, until almost 21 months after Heinkel's He 178 had taken to the air.

Me 262 VICTORIES

Some 1430 Me 262s were to be produced, in seven main versions, but probably no more than a third of them actually saw combat (and over 100 were lost, many in accidents on landing) over a seven-month period. By the spring of 1945 they were operating under very difficult circumstances but were still downing American bombers in significant numbers, particularly when equipped with 5.5cm R4M 'Orkan' ('Hurricane') unguided rocket projectiles, despite a never-cured tendency to snake at high speed, which made aiming somewhat unpredictable. The total number of victories scored by Me 262s is uncertain, but is authoritatively put at more than 735. The highest-scoring pilot was Oberleutnant Kurt Welter, with over 20 victories, and 27 other Luftwaffe pilots became jet aces, with five or more victories each, including

Below: The Me 262B-1 night-fighters of 10/NJG 11 were assigned to the defence of Berlin. One of the unit's pilots, Feldwebel Karl-Heinz Becker, accounted for seven Allied aircraft. Note the radar array on the nose.

MESSERSCHMITT Me 262B-1a/U1
Type: Two-seat night-fighter
Length: 11.53m (37.83ft)
Span: 12.48m (40.96ft)
Max take-off weight: 6585kg (14,515lb)
Max speed: 813km/h (505mph) at 6000m (19,700ft)
Range: 1050km (652 miles)
Armament: 4 x MK 108 30mm cannon

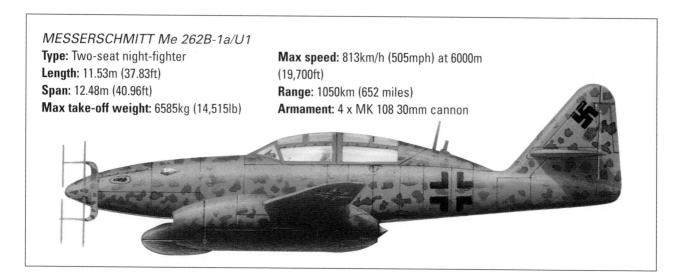

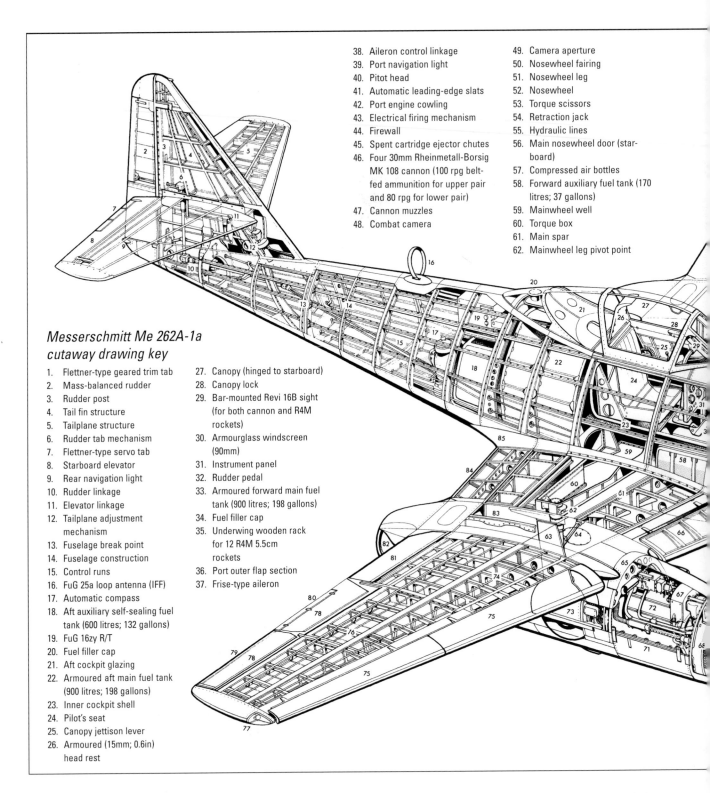

**Messerschmitt Me 262A-1a
cutaway drawing key**

1. Flettner-type geared trim tab
2. Mass-balanced rudder
3. Rudder post
4. Tail fin structure
5. Tailplane structure
6. Rudder tab mechanism
7. Flettner-type servo tab
8. Starboard elevator
9. Rear navigation light
10. Rudder linkage
11. Elevator linkage
12. Tailplane adjustment mechanism
13. Fuselage break point
14. Fuselage construction
15. Control runs
16. FuG 25a loop antenna (IFF)
17. Automatic compass
18. Aft auxiliary self-sealing fuel tank (600 litres; 132 gallons)
19. FuG 16zy R/T
20. Fuel filler cap
21. Aft cockpit glazing
22. Armoured aft main fuel tank (900 litres; 198 gallons)
23. Inner cockpit shell
24. Pilot's seat
25. Canopy jettison lever
26. Armoured (15mm; 0.6in) head rest

27. Canopy (hinged to starboard)
28. Canopy lock
29. Bar-mounted Revi 16B sight (for both cannon and R4M rockets)
30. Armourglass windscreen (90mm)
31. Instrument panel
32. Rudder pedal
33. Armoured forward main fuel tank (900 litres; 198 gallons)
34. Fuel filler cap
35. Underwing wooden rack for 12 R4M 5.5cm rockets
36. Port outer flap section
37. Frise-type aileron

38. Aileron control linkage
39. Port navigation light
40. Pitot head
41. Automatic leading-edge slats
42. Port engine cowling
43. Electrical firing mechanism
44. Firewall
45. Spent cartridge ejector chutes
46. Four 30mm Rheinmetall-Borsig MK 108 cannon (100 rpg belt-fed ammunition for upper pair and 80 rpg for lower pair)
47. Cannon muzzles
48. Combat camera

49. Camera aperture
50. Nosewheel fairing
51. Nosewheel leg
52. Nosewheel
53. Torque scissors
54. Retraction jack
55. Hydraulic lines
56. Main nosewheel door (starboard)
57. Compressed air bottles
58. Forward auxiliary fuel tank (170 litres; 37 gallons)
59. Mainwheel well
60. Torque box
61. Main spar
62. Mainwheel leg pivot point

Generalleutnant Adolf Galland, who formed and then commanded the ad hoc unit known as 'Jagdverband 7' after being implicated in the January 1945 'revolt' of Luftwaffe fighter unit leaders.

Was the Messerschmitt Me 262 worth the time and effort it took to develop, when all was said and done? The answer is a qualified 'yes', but the situation, most experts agree, would have been very different had the two major hold-ups – the late delivery of the engines and the Führer's meddling – been somehow speedily dealt with. Had the Luftwaffe's fighter squadrons been able to operate it in significant numbers from, let's say, mid-1944, the outcome would probably have been very different. It would not have won the war for

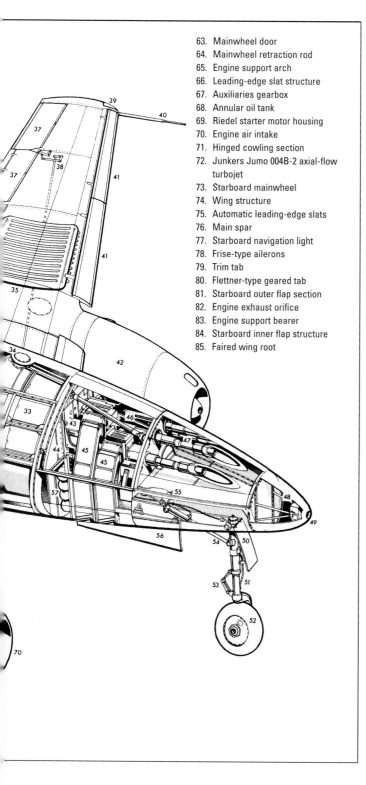

63. Mainwheel door
64. Mainwheel retraction rod
65. Engine support arch
66. Leading-edge slat structure
67. Auxiliaries gearbox
68. Annular oil tank
69. Riedel starter motor housing
70. Engine air intake
71. Hinged cowling section
72. Junkers Jumo 004B-2 axial-flow turbojet
73. Starboard mainwheel
74. Wing structure
75. Automatic leading-edge slats
76. Main spar
77. Starboard navigation light
78. Frise-type ailerons
79. Trim tab
80. Flettner-type geared tab
81. Starboard outer flap section
82. Engine exhaust orifice
83. Engine support bearer
84. Starboard inner flap structure
85. Faired wing root

Left: Despite its revolutionary wing form, the Me 262 was constructed along entirely conventional lines, the only limiting factor of the powerplant being the need to keep the airframe components out of the exhaust stream.

THE Ar 234 'BLITZ'

The only other jet-propelled German aircraft to see serious combat during World War II came not from one of the major manufacturers, but from a relatively minor player. Prior to the development of the Ar 234 'Blitz' ('Lightning') bomber (also known as the 'Hecht' – 'Pike'), the Arado company had only ever been involved in the production of light aircraft. Many of them, such as the Ar 196, were produced as floatplanes, designed to operate from warships, though that is not to say that its products were anything less than excellent. In 1940, the RLM issued a specification for a high-speed reconnaissance aircraft to be powered by two jet engines, either Jumo 004s or BMW 003s. Arado responded with a design – the E.370 – for a shoulder-wing monoplane with engines in under-slung nacelles, which was accepted as the Ar 234. Two prototypes were constructed over the winter of 1941–42, but it was February 1943 before the first pair of engines, the Jumo 004Bs, were delivered, and 15 June before the aircraft first flew. It was entirely conventional for the period, save in one respect: the fuselage was very slim and instead of a wheeled undercarriage, it used a take-off trolley and landed on skids. This was clearly unacceptable in an operational aircraft since it made manoeuvring on the ground next to impossible, so midway through the prototype programme, the fuselage was marginally widened beneath the wings, and main wheels and a retractable nosewheel were installed. Arado engineers also developed a rocket-powered interceptor, the E.381, which was to have been carried as a parasite beneath the fuselage of the Ar 234. Nothing came of the idea.

Most of the early Ar 234s were completed as reconnaissance aircraft, and flew many successful missions at 700km/h (435mph) at between 9000m (29,530ft) and 12,000m (41,000ft), where they were largely immune to attack, but a bomber version with either one or two seats, and able to carry 2000kg (4400lb) of bombs, was also produced. It was February 1945 before the first of these aircraft, assigned to KG 76, were operational. One was shot down by American P-47 Thunderbolts near Segelsdorf on 24 February, and fell into Allied hands. The most important missions KG 76 undertook were those aimed at the destruction of the Ludendorff Bridge over the

Germany, but it might well have prolonged it by some months by making inroads into the Allies' (especially the Americans') strategic bombing campaign, thus helping to maintain German manufacturing production levels. The question of whether that would have been a good or a bad thing lies outside the scope of this work.

Rhine at Remagen between 7 and 17 March, when Ar 234s made repeated and often suicidal attacks supported by Me 262 bombers of KG 51. A night-fighter version of the Ar 234 was produced in small numbers, and operated from March 1945 with some success. Later Ar 234 variants had a variety of different powerplants, and a four-engined version using 'siamesed' nacelles was also produced in prototype. Maximum speed at medium level of the latter was over 850km/h (530mph), which was beyond the level-flight capabilities of any Allied fighter, but still by no means fast enough for absolute safety. The limiting factor on its performance was not, however, the engines: it was the design of the wing. Straight wings have a finite maximum speed, after which compression causes local airflow to exceed the speed of sound, resulting in potentially catastrophic instability. Arado's engineers discovered this the hard way, but soon designer Rüdinger Kosin came up with an alternative planform: a crescent wing, starting out with its leading edge sweeping back from the wing roots, the curve returning so that the wingtip sections were at right-angles to the body axis (a form which was later used in the British Handley-Page 'Victor' bomber). Wind tunnel tests showed this to be much more effective, but the war ended before a prototype could be constructed. And even while the Ar 234 was in development, engineers elsewhere were looking at much more advanced concepts.

Left: The Arado Ar 234 – this is the production-B variant – with its long, slim fuselage and wings, was the only real alternative to the Me 262, but was nowhere near as successful in operational terms.

THE JUNKERS Ju 287

There is no space here to go into the complex aerodynamics of wing form in any depth, save to say that as early as the mid-1930s, it had been accepted – following the work of the *Deutsches Versuchsanstalt für Luftfahrt* (DVL – the German Aviation Development Establishment) – that straight wings had a finite speed limit thanks to the rise in drag caused by air compressing at their leading edge. As we have seen, this was the main factor in limiting the speed of the Ar 234. An interim solution was to sweep the leading edge backwards but keep the trailing edge straight, thus producing a variable-chord wing, and this was adopted with piston- and jet-engined aircraft alike. The Me 262 had a wing essentially of this form (although it did have a small sweep to its trailing edge outboard of the engines) as did the altogether more pedestrian Douglas C-47/DC-3 transport. At this time, no aircraft had flown with a wing that had steeply swept leading and trailing edges, even though it was known from wind tunnel testing that such a wing would benefit not only from decreased compressibility but also from a reduction in the ratio between its thickness and its chord (the distance between the leading and trailing edges).

In June 1943, at about the time when the Arado Ar 234 first flew, a development team at Junkers, under Dr Hans Wocke, produced a design for an advanced bomber using a double-swept wing form, but with one

Below: A total of 210 examples of the Arado Ar 234B were produced; just one remains, on display in the Smithsonian Institution's National Air and Space Museum in Washington D.C.

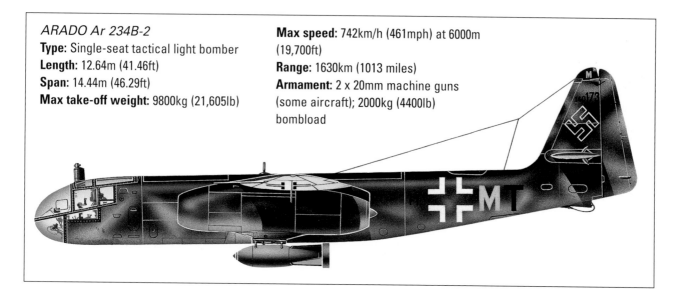

ARADO Ar 234B-2
Type: Single-seat tactical light bomber
Length: 12.64m (41.46ft)
Span: 14.44m (46.29ft)
Max take-off weight: 9800kg (21,605lb)

Max speed: 742km/h (461mph) at 6000m (19,700ft)
Range: 1630km (1013 miles)
Armament: 2 x 20mm machine guns (some aircraft); 2000kg (4400lb) bombload

Above: Surrounded by Junkers Ju 88Gs, this Ar 234B was captured by US forces at Manching in Bavaria in April 1945. The state of its cockpit bears out the assertion that the full glazing offered no protection against flying debris.

further innovation. The wing was to be swept not back, but forward, conferring all the advantages outlined above but also resulting in greater stability, except under certain well-defined circumstances. Wocke's project was championed by Siegfried Kneymeyer who was already a leading advocate of the abandonment of all piston-engined aircraft manufacture (save for the Junkers Ju 88) in the Reich.

A CHANGE AT THE TOP

In November 1943, Kneymeyer took over from Ernst Udet as Chief of Technical Air Armament at the RLM, and thus had considerable influence. The following March, prototype development of Wocke's new aircraft, designated the Ju 287, was ordered, and construction of a flying testbed began, using the fuselage of a Heinkel He 117. It was to be powered by

Above: The Ar 234B was found to be underpowered, and the obvious solution was to double up on the powerplants to produce the Ar 234C. Both reconnaissance and night-fighter versions were built alongside the bomber variant.

four 004B engines of 900kg (1984lb) thrust each, two suspended from the wings, the other two mounted on the fuselage sides, just below and aft of the cockpit. It would have two Walter 501 rockets to assist take-off.

The prototype aircraft made its maiden flight on 16 August and proved to be predictable in flight, though wing flexing was more of a problem than had been anticipated and when it yawed the trailing wing tend-ed to lift and create a rolling moment. On the whole, however, results were positive, and work went ahead on the construction of a second prototype with a pur-pose-built fuselage, to be powered by six BMW 003 turbojets, four wing-mounted and two mounted on the fuselage. In July, however, a new *Führerdirectiv* insti-gated the *Reichsverteidigungs* programme, which ordered all development work not concerned with

Below: An early Ar 234 screeches down the runway as it lands on its skids. Such a landing arrangement was out of the question for operational purposes, so the fuselage was widened and main wheels and a nosewheel fitted.

Above: The Junkers Ju 287, with its forward-swept wings and nose-mounted engines, was one of the more radical aircraft of World War II. This is the sole example built, the -V1 prototype. It was later captured by Soviet troops.

fighters and interceptors to be stopped, and accordingly no further progress was made with the Ju 287 V2, though the Ju 287 V1 continued to fly occasional tests. In March 1945, the project was suddenly revived and the Ju 287 ordered into production. Construction of the Ju 287 V2 recommenced, and plans were made for a -V3, with a pressurised three-man cockpit, 4000kg (8800lb) bombload, and remotely controlled guns, to be powered by four Heinkel 011 engines of 1300kg (2866lb) thrust. Two Jumo 012 engines of 2780kg (6120lb) thrust or two BMW 018 engines of 3400kg (7480lb) thrust (neither of which had actually been completed) were posited as an alternative. Both the Ju 287 V1 and the still-incomplete -V2 fell into Soviet hands in May 1945; the former

was flown as found, while the latter was completed with swept-back wings and is said to have achieved speeds of around 1000km/h (620mph). Hans Wocke later produced a civil aircraft, the HFB 320 'Hansa', with a swept-forward wing.

THE He 162 'SPATZ'/'SALAMANDER'

By 1944, with the situation looking increasingly black for Germany, there was a vocal school of thought which advocated the development of almost disposable weapons, to be used, in the last resort, by barely trained personnel. Rather more practical was a design which Heinkel produced in response to an RLM requirement for the *Volksjäger* (People's Fighter), a cheap and expendable fighter aircraft weighing less than 2000kg (4400lb), to be powered by a single BMW 003 jet engine, with an endurance of 30 minutes and an armament of two 30mm cannon. This craft was to be flown by volunteers from the Hitlerjugend. Design studies were 'invited' from Arado,

Blohm & Voss, Focke-Wulf, Junkers, Heinkel and Messerschmitt on 8 September 1944, to be considered a week later; the prototype aircraft was to fly before the year's end.

Only Messerschmitt declined the invitation. The Blohm & Voss design (P.211) was considered the best, but for some reason, the Heinkel submission (P.1073) was chosen, placing the engine in a nacelle mounted atop the fuselage; the engine discharged its exhaust between twin rudders, and by that means avoided all the problems of intake and exhaust ducting. By 23 September, a mock-up had been built and work began on the prototype the following day (six days before an official order was delivered). By 29 October a set of final drawings had been produced. Almost amazingly, the prototype flew for the first time on 6 December – three weeks before the deadline – but on a second flight on 10 December it crashed during a high-speed low-level pass, killing its pilot, Flugkapitän Peters, when the starboard wing disintegrated. It was later discovered that a fault in the formulation of the phenolic resin used to bond the plywood from which the wings were fabricated had caused the failure.

By the year's end, a variety of faults in stability had shown up in the second prototype, though these were all cured by mid-January (even if only to the point where an experienced pilot could fly the aircraft; it was still very much of a handful for a novice, though the same was true of the Me 262). By the end of the month, weapons' testing had shown that it would be necessary to replace the 30mm MK 108 with the 20mm MK 151. With that, the Heinkel 162 'Spatz' ('Sparrow', as it was called within the firm; it

Above: The Heinkel He 162, the 'People's Fighter', was to have been operated by barely trained volunteers from the ranks of the Hitler Youth, but it proved very difficult to fly.

later became known semi-officially as the 'Salamander') went into production at most of the existing Junkers and Heinkel factories (where the duralumin semi-monocoque fuselage was constructed) and in small furniture factories, where the wings and tail assemblies were produced. Final assembly took place at the Heinkel works at Rostock-Marienehe, at the Junkers works at Bernburg, and at the vast underground factory of 'Mittelwerke GmbH' near Nordhausen. Once again, it was too late, of course, though some 275 aircraft were actually completed and around 800 more were ready for assembly. The *Volksjäger* rarely saw combat, though it was claimed that

Below: The He 162A was straight winged, but designs were drawn up for a version with swept-back wings and another with forward-swept wings. Neither was built.

HEINKEL He 162
Type: Single-seat interceptor fighter
Length: 9.05m (29.71ft)
Span: 7.20m (23.625ft)
Max take-off weight: 2700kg (5952lb)

Max speed: 835km/h (519mph) at 6000m (19,700ft)
Range: 1000km (620 miles)
Armament: 2 x 30mm MK 108 or
2 x 20mm MG 151 cannon

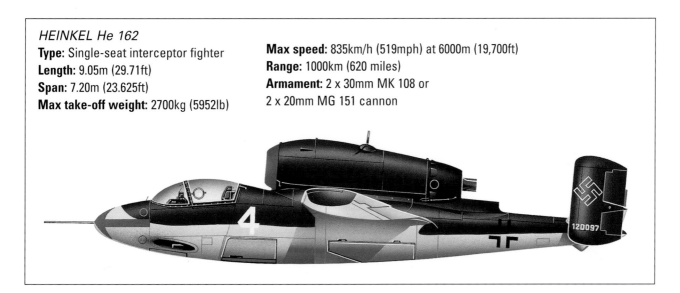

one aircraft – in the hands of Leutnant Rudolf Schmitt of 1/JG 1 based at Leck near the Danish border in Schleswig-Holstein – did shoot down a low-flying RAF Typhoon on 4 May 1945 (the claim was not allowed; the credit went to a nearby flak unit instead) and one was shot down, killing the pilot. Nine other members of JG 1 died and five were injured in flying accidents during conversion from the Fw 190; the He 162 was still very unforgiving. Post-war evaluation by Allied air forces indicated that with a little more development work, it would have been entirely viable, however, and would almost certainly have made a considerable impact, if only it had been available 12 – or even 6 – months earlier.

THE EMERGENCY FIGHTER PROGRAMME

Expedients like the *Volksjäger* were not the only option under consideration in mid-1944. It was becoming increasingly obvious to the Luftwaffe's

Below: He 162 components were manufactured all over Germany and sent to three central locations for assembly. In all, some 275 aircraft were completed, and components for around 800 more were on hand at the war's end.

High Command that it had effectively missed the boat, and that the jet and rocket-powered fighters which were about to enter service would soon be ineffective against a new generation of Allied aircraft such as the B-29 Superfortress with its 11,000m (36000ft) plus ceiling. Just before the end of the year, Kneymeyer issued a specification for a new generation fighter to all the principal producers, with the stipulation that the aircraft should be powered by the HeS 011 engine. Roughly, the performance parameters were a top speed in-level flight of around 1000km/h (620mph) at 7000m (23,000ft) and a ceiling of 14,000m (45,900ft); it was to be armed with four MK 108 30mm cannon. By February 1945, three proposals had been received from Messerschmitt, two from Focke-Wulf and one each from Blohm & Voss, Heinkel and Junkers. On the last day of the month, a selection committee sat and chose Focke-Wulf's Project I to go into development as the Ta 183.

THE FOCKE-WULF Ta 183

The two projects from Kurt Tank's design department were the work of a man who has been described as the most important aerodynamicist in Germany at the time, Hans Multhopp. They were essentially similar in character: a fuselage which was no more than a shroud for the single engine, its intake duct and exhaust tube, with the pressurised cockpit and weaponry sited above it, which was to be supported on stubby swept-back shoulder wings (constant-chord in Project I, variable-chord in Project II), with a tail unit cantilevered out behind. The tail unit itself was the factor which differentiated the designs. That of Project I was entirely innovatory: a T-tail, with the horizontal control surfaces located at its upper end; that of Project II was conventional, with the tailplane located low down. Otherwise, considerable attention was paid to ease of manufacture with the sort of resources which could be expected to be available, and the result of that was a projection that each aircraft would require a total of 2500 man-hours (the Me 262 probably never got far below 10,000). No single Ta 183 was ever built, Focke-Wulf's factories having been overrun by late April, but it is widely held that the Soviet Army took a complete set of plans, and the design team of Mikoyan and Gurevich is said to have used them as the basis for the MiG-15, powered by a Russian copy of the British Rolls-Royce 'Nene' turbojet engine. SAAB in Sweden later produced a very similar-looking aircraft as its SAAB-29, this time powered by a copy of the de Havilland 'Ghost'.

THE MESSERSCHMITT P. 1101

Another of the aircraft entered for the Emergency Fighter Competition was also to form the basis of a type built elsewhere, but this time rather more openly. The Messerschmitt company had in fact anticipated the need for a replacement for the Me 262 (who was in a better position to know that aircraft's limitations?) and construction of a prototype to replace it, designed by Woldemar Voigt, had begun in July 1944 as the P. 1101. This was in one particular a remarkable aircraft, for it was constructed chiefly to determine the best angle of wing sweep; its variable-chord wings could be reset (on the ground, not in flight) to any angle between 35 and 45 degrees. Otherwise, the aircraft was conventional in the new mould, with a single engine located deep within the fuselage and exhausting below the extension boom which supported the tail assembly.

The prototype was about 80 per cent complete when it was discovered by the Americans on their arrival in Oberammergau, and it was put on display in the open along with other 'interesting' developments from the Messerschmitt studio. It was still there, deteriorating rapidly, when it was spotted by Robert Woods, Chief Designer at Bell Aircraft, who contrived to have it sent it to the United States, where it was eventually restored and completed, with the help of Voigt himself, as a non-flying mock-up. It formed the basis for the first ever variable-geometry-winged aircraft, the Bell X-5, the sweep angle of which could be changed in flight to one of three pre-sets: 20, 40 and 60 degrees. This aircraft made its first flight on 20 June 1951, the geometry of the wing being varied in flight for the first time on 15 July.

THE MESSERSCHMITT P. 1110 AND P. 1111

The other two submissions Messerschmitt made were less well developed but somewhat more radical. The P. 1110 did away with the nose air intake, locating the engine much further back in the airframe, with the duct openings on the fuselage shoulders, just forward of the trailing edges of the constant-chord swept wings. The P. 1111 was more adventurous: an all-wing design of near-delta planform with a heavily swept tail fin and rudder, the air intakes of which were located in the forward part of the wing roots. A proposal submitted too late for the competition was a variant of this design, with a wing of narrower chord and a butterfly tail. Under ideal circumstances, all three designs would probably have been built in prototype form and flown against each other, but as it

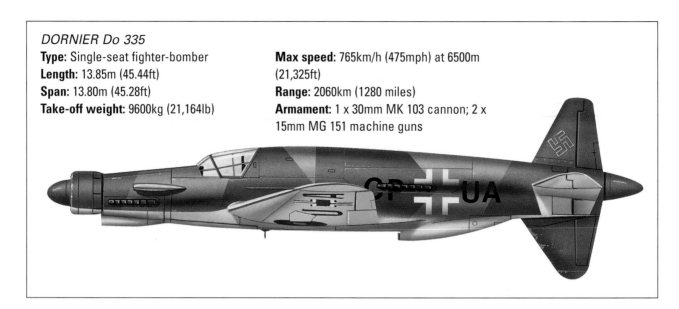

DORNIER Do 335
Type: Single-seat fighter-bomber
Length: 13.85m (45.44ft)
Span: 13.80m (45.28ft)
Take-off weight: 9600kg (21,164lb)

Max speed: 765km/h (475mph) at 6500m
(21,325ft)
Range: 2060km (1280 miles)
Armament: 1 x 30mm MK 103 cannon; 2 x
15mm MG 151 machine guns

was, none ever progressed beyond a partially completed wooden mock-up.

THE OTHER CONTENDERS

The other submissions to the Emergency Fighter Competition were all tailless designs too, which goes to show, perhaps, how far that concept had been accepted in Germany by the end of 1944. Of these designs, Blohm & Voss's P. 212 was perhaps the most radical, with twin stubby fins and rudders at the wingtips, supporting a winglet – half a tailplane, in fact – the rear surfaces of which formed elevators and also acted as additional ailerons. Like all Blohm & Voss's late wartime designs, the P. 212 was the work of the Director of Development, Dr Richard Vogt, who is credited with something like 200 different ideas for new aircraft, virtually none of which even made it to prototype. The design Heinkel submitted as P. 1078C was for a more straightforward flying wing. The wing itself was to have had considerable anhedral, with the tips turned down through 40 degrees over their last 50cm (20in) or so.

The Junkers P. 128 had a more conventional wing planform, wider but with a narrower aspect-ratio and set at shoulder height, although it had its engine intake ducts located under the wing at about halfway through their chord length. It had finlets with rudders, located about halfway between wing root and wingtip, which protruded both above and below the wing surface. All this was the work of Heinrich Hertel, a comparative newcomer to Junkers who, until 1939, had worked with Heinkel on the He 176 and the He 178. He left Heinkel largely, we are told, because he had little faith in rocket power, so it was somewhat

Above: Besides its 30mm forward-firing cannon and 15mm machine guns, the Do 335 could carry a 1000kg (2200lb) bombload, half in its weapons bay and half on hardpoints situated beneath its wings.

ironic that he was given the job of re-designing the Me 163 'Komet' (qv) to produce the Ju 248.

Cursory though this analysis has been, we have touched upon all the major German aircraft manufacturers save two: Dornier and Henschel. Claudius Dornier was, if anything, more conservative than even Tank or Hugo Junkers, and would have nothing to do with jet propulsion. His main contribution to aviation innovation lay in his development of a twin-engined fighter-bomber with its powerplants in a single axis:

Below: The Dornier Do 335 'Pfeil' was potentially the fastest piston-engined aircraft ever built, with one 1800bhp Daimler-Benz DB 603 engine in the nose and another in the tail.

Above: Total production of the 'Pfeil' ('Arrow') remained small, but that did not prevent the German Air Ministry from ordering prototypes in configurations to satisfy a variety of roles.

one in the nose, driving a tractor propeller; the other in the tail, driving a pusher. The Do 335 'Pfeil' ('Arrow', known unofficially as the 'Ameisenbär' – 'Anteater') was potentially the fastest piston-engined aircraft ever built, yet still exhibited most of the manoeuvrability of a single-engined fighter. It showed no bad manners when flying on only one engine, and could even take off with one inoperative. The only drawback to the arrangement was that it required special measures to abandon the aircraft in an emergency. The rear propeller and upper tail fin were jettisoned, then the canopy was blown off before the pilot could attempt to bale out (though at least one example was fitted with an ejection seat, the first in operational service). Initially, there was considerable resistance to its development from the RLM for the somewhat inconclusive reason that Dornier built not fighters but bombers, and the company had to under-

take to build an intruder version before permission to continue with the project was forthcoming. The first prototype made its maiden flight in September 1943, powered by two 1800hp DB 603 engines. By the end of the war, a version with 2100hp engines was flying. Several proposals were in process of consideration at the war's end, including swapping the rear engine for an HeS 011 turbojet and linking two aircraft together by means of a short central wing section, like the Heinkel He 111Z 'Zwilling' ('Twin'; see Chapter Three). Henschel's most important work was to be done in the field of guided weapons, though the company did propose a turbojet-powered dive-bomber,

Above: Despite its appearance, the Heinkel He 177 was actually a four-engined bomber – each nacelle housed a pair of Daimler-Benz DB 601 engines, each producing 1000bhp, linked to a single propeller.

the Hs 132, which was very well received by RLM. It was somewhat similar in form to the He 162, with a single turbojet mounted in a nacelle above the fuselage and a similar tail assembly (the similarities were not accidental), with a narrow-diameter cigar-shaped fuselage just big enough to accept a pilot in the prone position. The company also worked on a contender for the Emergency Fighter Competition, the Hs 135, with a compound delta wing like that later incorporated into the SAAB 'Draken'.

THE GERMAN HEAVY BOMBERS

Of course, jet and rocket engines powered only a small minority of the new aircraft produced in Germany during World War II. Most of them had 'conventional' piston engines, but the development of these aircraft, too, was far from smooth. During the first three years of the war, at least, German aero-engine manufacturers failed to come up with really powerful piston engines and that caused airframe designers to adopt some quite novel solutions to the problem of attaining high performance levels, both in fighter aircraft and in the elusive heavy/strategic bomber development programme.

Even though the Luftwaffe was a tactical, close-support air force, there was a programme aimed at developing a strategic bomber during the early years of the Third Reich. This resulted in the development of aircraft such as the Junkers Ju 89/Ju 90 and the stillborn Dornier Do 19, but it died with the Luftwaffe Chief of Staff, General Wever, in a plane crash on 3 June 1936, and was not resurrected until halfway through World War II. Even at that relatively late date, there was no suitable powerplant available for aircraft capable of carrying a 2000kg (4400lb) bombload to a target 1600km (1000 miles) away at a speed of 500km/h (310mph), and the solution adopted was to couple two engines together to turn a single propeller. The choice fell on the 1000bhp DB 601, linked to form the DB 606 (and later variants had more power, culminating in the DB 613, which had 3600hp available for take-off, with water injection and emergency boost). It was a far from satisfactory solution, and for a long time, the 'siamesed' engines tended to overheat and first vaporise and then ignite petrol in adjacent fuel tanks, with disastrous results.

Both the most important heavy bomber projects – the Heinkel He 177 'Greif' ('Griffon') and the Junkers Ju 288C – had pairs of siamesed engines as their powerplant. They were designed to carry both conventional bombloads in internal bays and external racks but also guided glider bombs such as the 'Fritz-X' or the Henschel Hs 293 (see Chapter Seven); odd suggestions for the Ju 288C included some other, more outlandish features, such as fitting it with the Düsenkanone 280 or the Gerät 104 'Münchhausen', single-shot guns of 28cm and 35.5cm calibre respectively (see Chapter Six). The Ju 388, which had even better performance, was planned as both a heavy bomber and a bomber destroyer, using Hs 298 and Ruhrstahl X-4 guided air-to-air missiles, and was also to have been employed in towing the Me 328 pulse-jet-boosted glider fighter to operational altitude. The only one built in significant numbers was the He 177, over 1000 of which were produced. One was modified to carry the German atomic bomb and many were fitted with forward-firing 5cm and 7.5cm anti-tank guns to be deployed on the Eastern Front. However, it was never entirely successful, even after five years of development. The Ju 288 did not get past the prototype stage. Some 65 Ju 388s of all types were built.

A high-altitude reconnaissance version of the He 177 was developed, powered by four (separate) DB 610 engines of 1750hp and with a new high aspect-ratio wing and a new twin fin tail. Known as the He 274, the prototype was built in Paris at the old Farman works, which were overrun in July 1944 before it could be completed. It was finished by the French and

Above: Like so many German aircraft projects, the He 177 was a case of 'too little, too late'. By the time it was ready to go into production, the Luftwaffe had little chance of operating a strategic bomber with any degree of success.

flown from December 1945. An improved version of the bomber, also with four separate engines and a twin fin tail, was built as the He 277, but only eight were completed before the Emergency Fighter Programme was put into effect on 3 July 1944.

THE 'AMERIKABOMBER'

Although they were developed in considerable secrecy, these aircraft do not really meet our criteria for secret weapons, though some 'conventional' piston-

Below: The sole example of the Me 264, the original 'Amerikabomber', first flew in December 1942. Such close attention was paid to its aerodynamic properties that the joints in the wings and fuselage were filled with putty.

engined bombers do. The Luftwaffe, we may recall, was intended as a tactical, rather than a strategic, air force, unlike the USAAF and the RAF, and it never operated really large, long-range bomber aircraft, like the American B-17 Flying Fortress or B-24 Liberator, or the British Lancaster, in any substantial numbers. It had aircraft, like the Focke-Wulf FW 200 'Condor' and the Junkers Ju 290 (though the former was designed as a civilian airliner and the latter was a hasty transformation of another), which were capable of flying very long distances, but these were intended primarily for ultra-long-range maritime reconnaissance, and while they did carry bombs (and variants of both carried glider bombs), they were unsuitable for use in combat conditions. Thus, when the USA declared war on Germany in December 1941, the Luftwaffe found itself without the means of attacking its new-found enemy, and the RLM immediately issued a specification for a suitable aircraft.

Three companies responded: Focke-Wulf with the Ta 400; Messerschmitt with the Me 264; and Junkers with the Ju 390. The Ta 400 was never built; the latter, which was little more than a Ju 290 stretched in wings and fuselage with two more engines, was reasonably straightforward, and the first prototype flew in August 1943. The second protype had a still longer fuselage and carried FuG 200 Hohentweil search radar and five 20mm cannon. On a test flight from Mont de Marsan on the Atlantic coast of France, near Bordeaux, it once approached to within 20km (12.4 miles) of New York before returning safely to base, thus validating the operational concept. A third prototype, this time a version able to carry 1800kg (3970lb) of bombs, was begun but never completed.

In fact, certain individuals at the RLM had begun to contemplate the possibility of bombing New York long before the United States entered the war, and Willy Messerschmitt for one had begun to think about a design for a suitable aircraft. His company was thus well placed to satisfy the requirement when it was issued in December 1941, and the prototype Me 264 made its first flight just 12 months later. With enough fuel to reach New York and return safely (a flight of anything up to 30 hours!), it could carry 3000kg (6600lb) of bombs, and still had enough capacity to carry 1000kg (2200lb) of armour plating. It had two complete three-man crews with a sleeping area and galley, and an elaborate defensive armament of four 13mm machine guns and two 20mm cannon. Under overload conditions, the aircraft could be fitted with up to six solid fuel rockets to assist it to take off. A

bewildering array of variants and variations were suggested, including one to tow an Me 328 glider fighter for protection, and another which would have been the flying testbed for a steam turbine powerplant. Two prototypes were begun; the first was destroyed in an air raid just as it was about to begin ground tests, but the second was completed and flew, being allocated to Transportstaffel 5, which operated other large aircraft types in the transport role. A version with greater wingspan and six engines was contemplated, but never produced. Thus the first round of the 'Amerikabomber' contest made no more than a token impact, but there was to be a second, as we shall see.

THE '3x1000' BOMBERS

Focke-Wulf, which produced the best German piston-engined single-seater fighter-bomber of the war, the Fw 190, had a genius in its Technical Director, Kurt Tank, but a very conservative one. As a result, the company was a latecomer to jet propulsion; too late, indeed, to see any Focke-Wulf jet fly in other than prototype form. One of those jets – the Fw Ta 183 (qv) – was to prove to be very influential indeed to post-war development. In 1943, however, the company did produce a series of designs to an in-house requirement known as '3x1000' for an aircraft to deliver a 1000kg (2200lb) bombload to a target 1000km (620 miles) away at a speed of 1000km/h (620mph). The first two designs had swept wings, one of variable chord and one of fixed chord, and a conventional tail assembly, but the third, which was much more radical in nature, was for a tailless 'flying wing', and shows very clearly the influence of Alexander Lippisch, who acted as a consultant to Tank from time to time. None of the designs was ever realised. Messerschmitt proposed a design to meet the same requirement, the P. 1107, which had moderately swept-back wings and a butterfly tail. Two basically similar designs were projected, the second of them with much greater range, but neither was realised.

THE HORTEN BROTHERS

The second of those two aircraft, the P. 1107B, would probably never have had trans-Atlantic range, but during the plan's currency the prospect of bombing the United States – which was now heavily involved in the war against Germany, on the ground in Italy and in the air from bases in the UK – reared up again. Once again, design proposals for an appropriate aircraft were solicited; this time a very different profile emerged, and one which shows just how far aerody-

Above: The first prototype of the Horten Ho IX was completed as a glider, but the second was fitted with twin Jumo 004B engines and logged speeds in excess of 800km/h (500mph). The Ho IX became the Gotha Go 229.

namics had progressed in Germany. The three main contenders were all of delta wing planform, which was clearly emerging as the shape of things to come, either with or without vertical tail surfaces. Alexander Lippisch was by no means alone in advocating it: the Horten brothers, Walter and Reimar, were just as committed and had been producing flying examples of delta wing aircraft, both gliders and powered aircraft, since the early 1930s.

The Hortens' first glider had been a wide delta, with its leading edge swept back at 24 degrees and its trailing edge straight, but the Ho II had its trailing edges swept back, too. Four examples of the latter were built as gliders, and then one was fitted with a 60hp Hirth motor driving a pusher propeller. Thanks to Walter Horten's friendship with Ernst Udet, the Luftwaffe procurement chief, this was put through a quasi-official trial at the hands of one of the best-respected test pilots of the day, Hanna Reitsch. She reported that its handling characteristics were favourable, that it was not vulnerable to spin or stall,

Above: Gotha engineers had misgivings about the ultimate stability of the Go 229, and planned to halt the programme. They were overtaken by events, however, and produced only one prototype, with four more under construction.

but that it was not very manoeuvrable. A series of designs, each better executed and more radical than the last (and each of them tailless), followed, and by the time of the Ho V, power had become the norm. By 1940, the Hortens were operating a Luftwaffe design studio known as 'Sonderkommando 9' at Göttingen, and soon produced plans for the Ho VIII (a 60-seat transport aircraft, powered by six pusher propellers), and the Ho IX, a turbojet fighter with twin Jumo 004B engines. The first prototype of the latter was completed as a glider, and the second as a powered aircraft. It was destroyed in an enforced single-engine landing, but not before it had logged speeds in excess of

800km/h (500mph). It was to go into production as the Gotha Go 229, with four MK 103 30mm cannon and a 1000kg (2200lb) bombload. Only one prototype, with the more powerful Jumo 004C engine, was completed before the war's end, though four more were begun. Calculations suggest that the Go 229 would have had a top speed of over 1000km/h (620mph) and indeed, it was presented to Hermann Göring as a contender for the '3x1000' project, but engineers at Gothaer Waggonfabrik were far from happy with its straight-line stability as it had a tendency to 'Dutch roll', yawing around the vertical Z axis while rolling from side to side around the X axis. The engineers planned to halt construction after the sixth prototype. The Hortens agreed, and produced a new design with a very pronounced, almost exaggerated, V-shaped fin, the leading edge of which came almost to the nose and included the cockpit. Lippisch

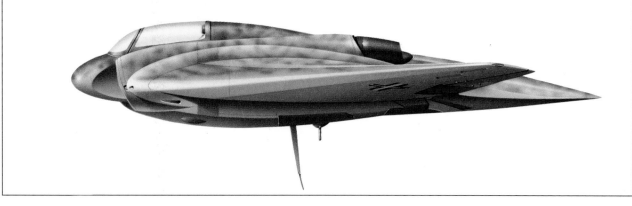

HORTEN Ho IX (GOTHA Go 229)
Type: Single-seat fighter-bomber
Length: 7.47m (24.51ft)
Span: 16.78m (55.05ft)
Max take-off weight: 8500kg (18,740lb)

Max speed (projected): 1000km/h (620mph) at 6100m (20,015ft)
Range: N/A
Armament (projected): 4 x 30mm MK 103 cannon; 2000kg (4400lb) bombload

Above: The Ho IX/Go 229 would probably have been capable of speeds in level flight in excess of 1000km/h (620mph), which would have made it by far the fastest production aircraft of its day.

produced several very similar designs. But the Hortens did not give up the tailless concept either, and also produced for a single-engine interceptor, though by the time they reached the third evolution, this, too, had become a delta with a conventional fin tail.

RE-ENTER THE 'AMERIKABOMBER'

By the time the Ho IX/Go 229 project was underway, the RLM had resurrected the 'Amerikabomber' programme, but the planemakers selected – Arado, Focke-Wulf, Heinkel, Junkers and Messerschmitt – had made little progress. Siegfried Kneymeyer then contacted the Hortens and asked them to turn their attention to a bomber with trans-Atlantic range. Not surprisingly, they came up with a flying wing, essentially an enlarged Ho IX, which they called the P. 18. All the would-be contenders were summoned to a conference at the RLM in February 1945, and the Horten design was selected for production. The brothers were instructed to work with designers from Junkers and Messerschmitt, but the proposed consortium soon fell apart when more conservative elements insisted on adding a large fin and hinged rudder to the design. Reimar Horten then went directly to Göring with a modified plan for the P. 18B, employing four HeS 011 engines in place of six Jumo 004s or BMW 003s, saving 1000kg (2200lb) with little loss of thrust. The aircraft, he confidently predicted, would have a

range of 11,000km (6835 miles) at 850km/h (530 mph) and fly at an altitude of 16,000m (52,500ft) with a 4000kg (8800lb) bombload. He was told to go ahead and build it, but by that time the war had only 10 weeks to run and it is doubtful whether detailed plans were drawn up, though they may have been later, as both brothers continued to work in aviation for the rest of their lives, Walter eventually becoming a leading light in the new Luftwaffe, Reimar in the aircraft industry in Argentina.

THE JUNKERS P. 130/P. 140

Junkers had, in addition to Hans Wocke, two other extremely talented designers in Ernst Zindel and Heinrich Hertel. These three soon responded to the new-found interest in all-wing aircraft and proposed one such of their own as Project 130. It is suggested that Hertel had produced the Ju 287 design only as a means of gaining experience in the sort of aerodynamics required by the P. 130, but it is worth bearing in mind that he had acquired some relevant experience with the Ju 322 (see Chapter Three). Similar in character to the Hortens' P. 18B, the P. 130 had a shorter range (around 5800km; 3600 miles), and was apparently intended to operate against targets in Soviet Asia and in England from bases in Prussia. The 'committee-modified' version of the P. 18A, with the addition of the long triangular tail fin, became the Junkers P. 140, with the range to carry 4.06 tonnes (4 tons) of bombs to New York. Like the P. 18B, it was ordered into production, but work had hardly begun before the underground factory in the Harz mountains where it was to have been built was overrun.

CHAPTER TWO

Rocket-powered Aircraft

Rocket-propelled interceptor aircraft were very attractive to the German Air Ministry, for they seemed to offer a realistic possibility of being able to threaten the high-flying Allied bombers which, by 1944, were decimating the country's industrial base. This was particularly true since they did not require fossil fuel, which was in very short supply by that time, and could be constructed cheaply, largely from plywood; a considerable effort was put into developing such aircraft, but ultimately to no avail.

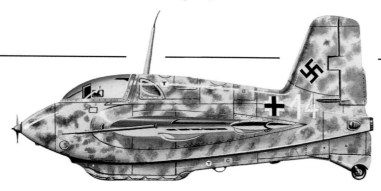

Had we been considering the history of thrust-powered flight in something like chronological order, rather than in terms of the impact the new technology had on the course of aviation in World War II, we would have examined the rocket before the jet. In fact, there is little conflict here, for the first effective demonstrations of the two types occurred almost simultaneously and in the same place: in the last months before the outbreak of war, at Ernst Heinkel's factory at Rostock-Marienehe. While neither type was actually conceived as a weapons platform, and even

Above: The Messerschmitt Me 163B-1 'Komet'.

Left: The Ba 349 had four solid-fuel booster rockets and a liquid fuel sustainer motor. Launched vertically, it was to have climbed to 14,000m (45,900ft) in one minute.

though neither did what was hoped of it, thanks to a series of poor design decisions, both demand inclusion here because of the influence – both positive and negative – they exerted. We have seen how the jet-propelled He 178 was deficient because its designer failed to solve the problem of how to induct air to the engine efficiently. This, it must be said, would have been hard to foresee. The main fault of the rocket-powered He 176, on the other hand, was glaringly obvious, at least to the cognoscenti. Unfortunately, there were few of them around in 1939.

THE HEINKEL He 176

The rocket-propelled aircraft designated the He 176 by the *Reichsluftfahrtministerium* (RLM – the German Air Ministry) was powered by a Walter R1 motor using hydrogen peroxide. Earlier versions (more accurately, existing He 112 fighters with auxiliary motors) had used a power unit developed by Wernher von Braun (qv), which used liquid oxygen and alcohol, a rather more volatile mixture. The near-explosive decomposition of hydrogen peroxide into superheated steam when it comes into contact with a catalyst such as calcium, potassium or sodium permanganate was to become a mainstay of German propulsion programmes in a number of very different areas, as we shall see. The He 176 flew for the first time on 30 June 1939. The aircraft probably never exceeded the standard it had been designed to beat, 700km/h (435mph), which was below the world speed record of the day. It was essentially too heavy both for its powerplant and for its short, stubby wings. The RLM showed little interest in it, favouring the design which would become the Messerschmitt Me 163 'Komet' (qv). Heinkel abandoned the project.

ALEXANDER LIPPISCH

Alexander Lippisch was a self-taught aerodynamicist who had worked at Zeppelin/Dornier after World War I, then at Rhön-Rossitten-Gesellschaft (RRG – which

Below: The Messerschmitt Me 163 'Komet' interceptor first went into action in August 1944. It accounted for only about a dozen Allied bombers in six or seven months.

developed gliders for meteorological research, amongst other things), and later, when RRG was absorbed into it, at the *Deutsches Forschungsinstitut für Segelflug* (DFS – German Glider Research Institute). Lippisch maintained that had Heinkel had even a narrow understanding of the nature of gliders, he would have realised that he needed a large wing area (and a small wing loading) to make an aircraft such as the He 176 fly adequately, as it had only very marginal power reserves. Instead, Heinkel had given his proto-rocket aircraft short, stubby wings which were really little more than control surfaces, and his experiments failed in direct consequence. Lippisch went further than that, of course. Like the Horten brothers, he was a staunch and unremitting advocate of the tailless, delta-planform flying wing, and was the first to fly such a design, in 1931. Three years before that, however, Lippisch had produced a rocket-propelled glider for automobile manufacturer Fritz von Opel, who saw the new technology mostly in terms of its ability to attract crowds, but who was interested enough (and rich enough) to provide seed money for would-be pioneers. Opel lost interest in the early 1930s, after rocket-powered gliders had been the death of a number of pilots. Lippisch's 'Ente' ('Duck') became the first rocket-powered aircraft to fly, with Fritz Stammer at the controls, on 11 June 1928. By 1933, Lippisch had designed a variety of

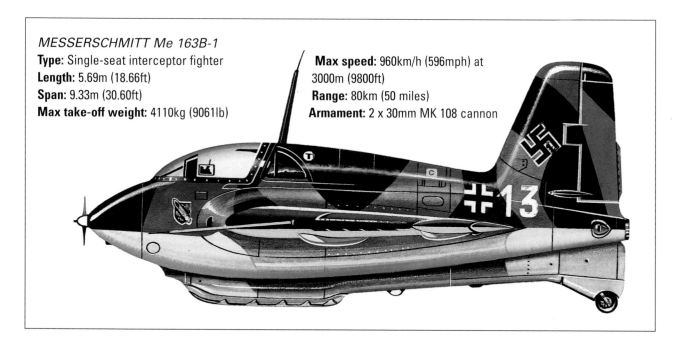

MESSERSCHMITT Me 163B-1
Type: Single-seat interceptor fighter
Length: 5.69m (18.66ft)
Span: 9.33m (30.60ft)
Max take-off weight: 4110kg (9061lb)

Max speed: 960km/h (596mph) at 3000m (9800ft)
Range: 80km (50 miles)
Armament: 2 x 30mm MK 108 cannon

delta-wing gliders and had begun to fit small engines to them. He collaborated with Focke-Wulf and with Gerhard Fieseler, and with the latter, built the two-seat, twin-engine (pusher and tractor) Delta III 'Wespe' ('Wasp') and Delta IV, only to see both crash at the cost of one pilot's life within a fortnight. RLM promptly banned tailless aircraft, and it was some time, and then only at the urging of Professor Walter Georgii, the Director of DFS, before the ban was lifted. A modified Delta IVb followed, with the RLM designation DFS 39, and in 1939, orders were issued for the construction of a version to be powered by a Walter rocket motor. DFS built the wings, which were of near-delta planform, and Heinkel built the rest of the airframe, alongside the He 176 with which it shared its powerplant. The design's concession to the RLM was the small wingtip rudders, but after wind-tunnel testing, Lippisch concluded that these would only cause flutter and, ultimately, main spar failure. Thus, the DFS 194, its successor, acquired a single, central fin and rudder. Using as its 'fuel' T-Stoff (an 80 per cent aqueous solution of hydrogen peroxide plus oxyquinoline as a stabiliser) and Z-Stoff (an aqueous solution of sodium and potassium permanganates to promote decomposition), the Walter RI-203 rocket was to propel the prototype at speeds of up to 500km/h (310mph). It was clear from the outset that this was a major achievement and Lippisch was ordered to Messerschmitt's Augsburg research centre with his research and development team in January 1939. There the DFS 194 metamorphosed into the Messerschmitt Me 163 'Komet' ('Comet').

Above: 'White 13' – an Me 163B-1a of 1/JG 400, which operated from near Leipzig between July 1944 and April 1945, defending the Leuna-Merseburg refinery complex.

THE Me 163 'KOMET'

The 'Komet', which preceded the jet-propelled Me 262 into service by a little over two months, was a radical and adventurous approach to the problem of how to defeat the heavily armed and protected bomber aircraft which were flown in formations designed to create an impenetrable defensive box. Its designation, all of them were decided by the RLM, is somewhat misleading, for Messerschmitt AG actually had little to do with its development, which remained in the hands of its creator. In the spring of 1941, the prototype of the new aircraft began gliding trials; towed to a height of up to 8000m (26,250ft), it was soon achieving speeds of up to 850km/h (530mph) while retaining a high degree of controllability, and during the summer it was sent to the rocket development establishment at Peenemünde-West on the Baltic coast, to be fitted with a rocket motor – an improved model of the Walter R1 incorporating a degree of thrust control but still using T-Stoff and Z-Stoff as its fuel. The development programme at Peenemünde was fraught with accidents, some fatal, as time after time the volatile fuels spontaneously exploded. On one occasion, an entire building was demolished. However, it also resulted in the Me 163 V1 breaking the world speed record repeatedly until the test pilot, Heini Dittmar, finally exceeded 1000km/h (620mph), almost killing himself in the

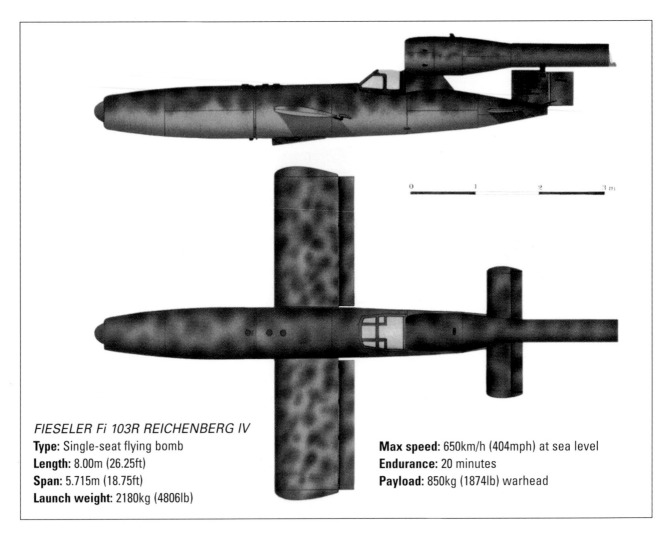

FIESELER Fi 103R REICHENBERG IV
Type: Single-seat flying bomb
Length: 8.00m (26.25ft)
Span: 5.715m (18.75ft)
Launch weight: 2180kg (4806lb)

Max speed: 650km/h (404mph) at sea level
Endurance: 20 minutes
Payload: 850kg (1874lb) warhead

Above: The Reichenberg IV, as the manned version of the V1 flying bomb was known, was little more than a fantasy, though prototypes did fly.

process when the aircraft became suddenly uncontrollable as compression shock (shocks caused by airflow over the wing surface locally exceeding the speed of sound) induced negative lift and massive vibration. In the event, Dittmar managed to regain control and land successfully. The RLM, impressed, ordered prototypes of an operational aircraft, the Me 163B, to be armed with a pair of MG 151 20mm cannon and powered by a more powerful 509-A2 rocket motor using the somewhat less unpredictable combination of T-Stoff and C-Stoff (30 per cent hydrazine hydrate, 57 per cent methanol, 13 per cent water) as its fuel and producing 1500kg (3300lb) of thrust. Around 2.032 tonnes (2 tons) of propellant (very nearly half the entire weight of the aircraft) was enough to take it to its operational ceiling of 12,100m (39,700ft) in 3.35 minutes, and the pilot then had a further four and a

half minutes of powered flight available: thus, he would actually have been gliding, unpowered, during most of his mission.

Two Me 163B-1as were handed over to a special Luftwaffe unit early in 1943 to allow pilot familiarisation to begin, though it was July before training actually commenced. The high landing speed of the 'Komet' (around 220km/h; 140mph) combined with the fact that the pilot was committed to it from the outset, having no power available to allow him to regain height for a second attempt, resulted in many accidents, most of them fatal. The first operational unit, equipped with Me 163B-1a aircraft, with a pair of 30mm cannon in the wing roots and a considerable degree of armour protection for the pilot, began forming at Wittmundhaven in May 1944, and first went into action as I/JG400 on 16 August. It scored its first success some days later, when Leutnant Hartmut Ryll downed a B-17 near Leipzig. In all, some 300 Me 163s in various versions were constructed (and rights to it were sold to Japan, where five powered and over

50 unpowered versions were built before the war's end), but the aircraft was only a very limited success, accounting, it is believed, for little more than 12 American B-17s. An improved version, known originally as the Ju 248, was produced at Junkers and then taken over by Messerschmitt as the Me 263. It was somewhat larger, had a wheeled undercarriage rather than skids, and was powered by a Walter 509C motor. It was produced in prototype form only.

THE SELBSTOPFERMÄNNER FIGHTERS

In fact, like the Me 262, the 'Komet' was too little, too late. So desperate was the situation in Germany by the summer of 1944 that individual fighter pilots had taken to ramming Allied bombers, and units such as IV/JG3 and II/JG300 were formed as *Sturmgruppen* (assault groups) with that as an accepted fall-back tactic using Fw 190A-8/R2s fitted with frontal armour. They had a measure of success: between 7 July 1944 and the end of March 1945, when they ceased to operate, they accounted for around 500 Allied bombers, but only 10 of them by ramming. In April 1945, Sonderkommando Elbe was formed from volunteers; they trained for 10 days in ramming tactics, and then went into action. In all, they rammed and downed eight, but at a high cost to themselves: a total of 77 Bf 109s and Fw 190s. If such potentially self-sacrificial *Selbstopfermänner* tactics were to be employed, then clearly a much less sophisticated aircraft, using little in the way of strategic materials, could be employed instead of some of the best piston-engined fighters of the entire period.

At this point we need to take a very short diversion to consider the nature of *Selbstopfermänner* tactics. It was never the stated intention to require or even ask aircrew to commit suicide in Germany in the way that it was in Japan, and great pains were taken to maintain that the very reverse was actually the case. The *Selbstopfermänner* were expected only to employ their aircraft as weapons in the last resort (though recruits to the *Sturmgruppen* were required to take an oath that they would indeed do this if necessary), and to make every effort to ensure that the attack left them with the possibility of escape. As will be noted when discussing the manned Fi 103s, the possibilities of this happening were remote, and it must be concluded that there was a secret agenda, and that the men

(and women; Hanna Reitsch was an advocate of such tactics) concerned knew exactly what they were being called upon to do, and that the disclaimers were there only for public relations purposes.

THE Ba 349 'NATTER'

The 'Komet' was hardly a sophisticated aircraft. However, according to Dr Erich Bachem the 'Komet' was over-sophisticated. Bachem was an experienced glider pilot and one-time Technical Director of Fieseler AG, which was latterly a manufacturer of wings for Henschel missiles and control surfaces for the A4 and where Bachem had designed the Fi 156 'Storch' ('Stork') observation and light utility aircraft. He claimed that a wooden glider, simple enough to have been built in a carpentry workshop and propelled by a similar rocket motor to that used in the 'Komet',

Right: The launch of the Ba 349 was so violent that the pilot was expected to black out; the climb to operational altitude was under a simple automatic guidance system.

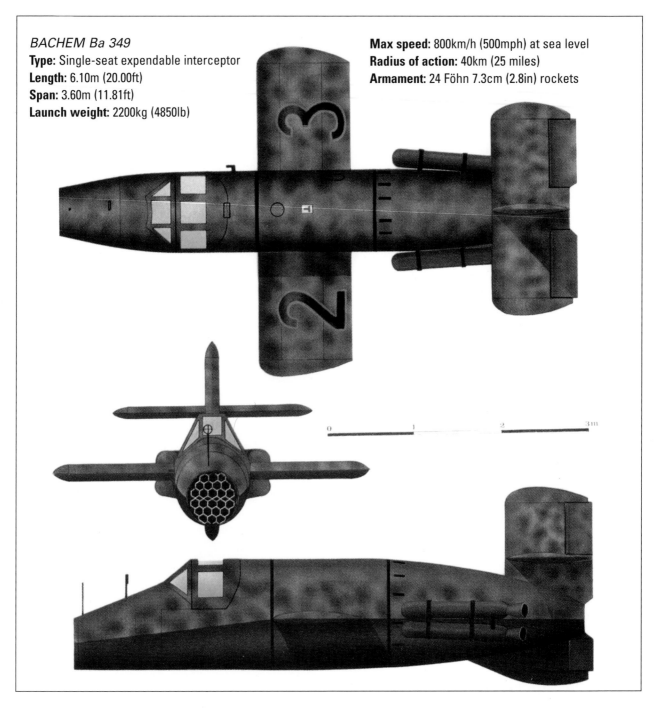

BACHEM Ba 349
Type: Single-seat expendable interceptor
Length: 6.10m (20.00ft)
Span: 3.60m (11.81ft)
Launch weight: 2200kg (4850lb)

Max speed: 800km/h (500mph) at sea level
Radius of action: 40km (25 miles)
Armament: 24 Föhn 7.3cm (2.8in) rockets

Above: The 'Natter' was conceived as the simplest means of getting a man within range of the high-flying bombers. The array of rockets in the nose were its sole weapons.

aided by four solid-fuel boosters so that it could take off vertically, would do the job equally well. It would climb to 14,000m (45,900ft) in little over a minute under control of a simple automatic guidance system, whereupon its pilot, by now hopefully having regained consciousness after blacking out under the forces generated at take-off, would take over and make a diving attack on the enemy bomber formation on his way back to earth. He would bale out to land by parachute only when he had fired his only armament (the 24 Henschel Hs 217 'Föhn' 7.3cm or R4M 5.5cm unguided rockets contained in an array in the nose), and had reduced his speed to around 250km/h (155mph), while the 'aircraft' from the cockpit back also descended by parachute in the hope of recovering the rocket motor for re-use. From 22 December 1944, a series of 11 unmanned launches were made on the power of the booster motors alone, and on 23

February 1945, a single, unmanned test launch took place using the Walter motor as well. Some days later a manned launch was ordered by the SS (*Schutzstaffeln*: the Nazis' private army) which, by that time, had control of all secret weapons projects, even though the unmanned programme had not been completed and there were grave doubts about the aircraft's viability. The pilot, one Lothar Siebert, was killed when the Ba 349 power-dived into the ground from a height of 1500m (4900ft) after having rolled on to its back. The testing programme continued, and perhaps 20 aircraft (some reports say 36) intended for operations were produced, but none flew in combat. It is thought that two examples remain, both in museum storage: one in the USA, the other in Germany.

Ernst Heinkel proposed a very similar aircraft to the Bachem 'Natter' ('Viper'). The P. 1077 'Julia' (it never received an RLM designator) was also to have been powered by a Walter 509 motor and four solid-fuel Schmidding 533 boosters. It was to have taken off from an inclined ramp, to climb to 15,000m (49,210ft) in 72 seconds, and to have been armed with two MK 108 cannon. It was a high-wing monoplane with almost square-planform wings with considerable anhedral at the tips, and drawings showing two different tail assemblies – one with a single dorsal fin and high-set stubby tailplanes; the other with a single high tailplane terminating in dorsal/ventral fins – were produced. It is probably better considered as a manned missile than an aircraft. There is no account of how the pilot was supposed to complete the mission and return safely to earth.

There is some question whether the 'Natter' actually fits our criteria for *Selbstopfermänner* aircraft at all, since the pilot was expected to break off his attack and turn for home before ejecting (indeed, he was provided with an escape system), but there is less doubt in similar concepts put forward by Zeppelin and DFS, both of which proposed what were essentially motor-assisted gliders to be towed into attack position by aircraft. The Zeppelin proposal – the 'Rammer' – had a solid-fuel rocket motor; the DFS aircraft, which went into development as the Messerschmitt Me 328, had an Argus pulse-jet like that which powered the Fieseler Fi 103 flying bomb (qv). There were high hopes of the latter, in particular, but like the Ba 349, it never got past the prototype stage. There was a third, very similar, project, the Sombold So 334 'Rammschussjäger', which, despite its name, was not actually intended to ram. It, too, was powered by the Walter 509 motor and armed with rockets, and

was to have been towed to operating height. Like the Me 328, it started out as a parasite escort fighter project but never got further than a wind tunnel model. Blohm & Voss proposed a pure glider fighter, with no powerplant at all, as the Bv 40. Armed with 30mm cannon and towing a proximity-fuzed bomb on a cable, the Bv 40 was to have been towed to a position above the incoming bomber 'box' by a Bf 109 and then released. Its limited acceptance was perhaps indicative of the state of mind in Germany by 1944 when prototypes were built and tested.

THE ZEPPELIN 'RAMMER'

The Zeppelin 'Rammer' never received an RLM designation, which is an indication that perhaps it was not taken entirely seriously. It was to have been a small conventional aircraft with straight, constant-chord wings and tailplane, and was to have been towed to its operational altitude by a Bf 109 or a Bf 110 and cast loose, whereupon it would start its Schmidding 533 solid-fuel rocket motor and head for the bomber formation, first firing its load of 14 R4M 5cm rockets and then trying to ram or sideswipe the bomber aircraft, using its hugely strong wings. The wing's leading edges were to have been covered in 3cm- (1.18in-) thick steel, and they were to have had three continuous parallel main spars, fabricated from thick-walled steel tubing, running from tip to tip to slice through fuselage, tailplane or wings. The pilot, who flew the aircraft in the prone position, was not expected to take to his parachute, but was to have landed the aircraft on any convenient piece of open ground so that it could be recovered and re-used. It is thought that no prototype nor even a mock-up of the 'Rammer' was actually constructed.

THE MESSERSCHMITT Me 328

The history of the Me 328 – which, like the 'Komet', started life as a DFS project – began in 1941, rather earlier than those of the other 'last-ditch' fighters. It was concieved as an escort fighter, to be towed by a Heinkel He 177 bomber on a semi-rigid bar (the 'Deichselschlepp' system, which was also under consideration for use with manned glider bombers and auxiliary fuel tanks) or mounted on a Dornier Do 217 or a Messerschmitt Me 264 in a 'Mistel'-like arrangement (qv). A variety of versions were projected: a pure glider; with Argus pulse-jets; and with a Jumo 004 turbojet. Only the pure glider and the pulse-jet versions were produced (and then only in prototype form). The ubiquitous Hanna Reitsch was responsible

Above: The Blohm & Voss Bv 40 was an unpowered glider and was to have been towed into position above the approaching bombers before making its attack.

for completing a test programme on the two proto-types of the glider version, cutting loose from tow planes at altitudes of 3000–6000m (9800–19,700ft). Ground launches, using both cable-type catapults and rocket-assisted rail carriages, were also undertaken, with equal success. Even with reduced wingspan, the aircraft performed very satisfactorily, and it was planned to build up to 1000 for use as disposable bombers, to be flown by volunteers from 5/KG200, the so-called 'Staffel Leonidas'.

Seven prototypes of the Argus pulse-jet-powered version were built by a glider maker, Jacob Schweyer Segelflugzeugbau. It was intended for use as a fighter aircraft, to be armed with two MG 151 machine guns. In static testing it soon became obvious that the same problems which were to plague the early development of the V1 flying bomb – notably, excessive vibration – would make the project difficult to bring to a suc-cessful conclusion, and the manned flight programme was suspended in mid-1944, after only a few test flights had been made. Nonetheless, planning still went ahead, and a version was projected, employing no less than four Argus 109-014 pulse-jets, two mounted below the mid-set wings in addition to the original pair mounted above the rear fuselage, their jet tubes protruding behind the fin below the tailplane.

Bomber versions of both these aircraft were also proposed (and would actually have made greater sense since the pulse-jet's characteristics were unsuit-ed to its use as a fighter powerplant). At Hitler's insis-tence, work on the bomber version continued long past the point when anything other than token use

Left: No more than 36 Ba 349s were constructed; none was ever sent into combat, and most finished like these three battered examples in the hands of GIs in Bavaria.

could have been made of it. Perhaps the most far-fetched suggestion for a version of the Me 328 was that with folding wings and twin pulse-jets, designed to be launched from a catapult set up on the foredeck of a submarine.

THE BLOHM & VOSS Bv 40

The simplest and cheapest – and perhaps the most sensible – proposal for a *Selbstopfermänner* fighter came from Blohm & Voss's Richard Vogt in mid-1943. The Bv 40 was a simple small armoured glider, armed with a pair of 30mm cannon and fitted with a considerable degree of frontal protection, constructed by unskilled workers from non-strategic materials, which was to have been towed to a position above the bomber formations by a Bf 109G and then cast loose to prosecute a head-on diving attack. One proposed innovation was the 'Gerät-Schlinge', which was real-ly nothing more than a towed aerial mine on a long cable, and which was to be exploded when it was within the bomber formation (although the bomb tended to trail directly behind the glider, rather than some way below it, and it was difficult to place as a result). R4M rockets and 250kg (550lb) bombs, to be dropped into bomber formations from above, were also suggested, as was a version to carry four aerial torpedoes. Six prototypes were constructed, and five flew before the project was cancelled in late 1944. In an attempt to resurrect it, Vogt suggested fitting it with Argus pulse-jets mounted under the wings, but he was unsuccessful, the Me 328 having taken up what small degree of enthusiasm existed for such a solution.

Hybrid Aircraft and Gliders

During World War II, Germany made extensive use of unpowered aircraft in the transport role, and though they met with diminishing success, they proved a useful addition to the Reich's logistical fleet. In a parallel development, technology developed for glider bombs was applied to the guidance of unmanned powered aircraft too, the flight to the vicinity of the target being under the control of the pilot of a single-engined fighter mounted piggyback on the explosives-packed bomber.

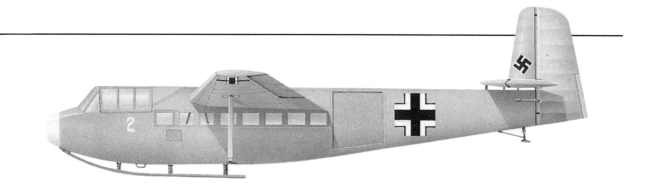

Even after the new German Air Force was established, the unpowered aircraft still occupied an important place in its order of battle, perhaps because almost all Luftwaffe pilots recruited before Germany openly re-armed had learned to fly in gliders. As we have seen, many important new developments in aviation sprang from the *Deutsches Forschungsinstitut für Segelflug* (DFS).

Above: The DFS 230 carried Luftwaffe paratroops into action against the Belgian fortress of Eben-Emael.

Left: The 'Mistel' was a fighter mated with an unmanned bomber, the nose of which was an explosive charge.

THE DFS 230

Gliders were eventually to be developed in Germany in all shapes and sizes and for a variety of roles. We have seen them as both bombers and fighters, but they were actually more effective, at least in combat terms, as troop carriers and transports. The first to see action was the diminutive DFS 230, a conventional glider with straight, high aspect ratio wings, developed from a prototype built by Rhön-Rossitten-Gesellschaft in 1932, which could carry eight combat-equipped soldiers. In a very real sense, the DFS 230 was a secret weapon par excellence, for in its combat debut, when Luftwaffe paratroopers used it to assault and capture the huge Belgian fortress at Eben-Emael on 10 May

1940, it achieved complete tactical and strategic surprise, and allowed the Wehrmacht to cross into Belgium virtually unopposed. Despite that success, once their existence was known, gliders proved to be an expensive way of getting infantry into combat, and after a near disaster in Crete, were not employed in that role by the Luftwaffe, although they were used in an even more dramatic way in September 1943, when commandos led by Otto Skorzeny landed 12 DFS 230s on a narrow strip of land in front of the Rifugio Hotel on the Gran Sasso and liberated deposed Italian dictator Benito Mussolini. From then on, it was left to the Allies to employ them, notably in Sicily in July 1943, in Normandy in June 1944, and at Arnhem in September of that year. That is not to say that the Luftwaffe had given up on them by any means.

THE DFS 228 AND DFS 346

DFS later built a single prototype of a cargo-carrying glider, the DFS 331, in 1941, but by that time the main thrust of the Institute's work lay in the development of high-performance experimental sailplanes. The most significant of those was the DFS 228, planned as a high-altitude photo-reconnaissance aircraft, to be transported to an altitude of 10,000m (32,800ft) or more and released, a rocket motor then taking it to an altitude of 23,000m (75,400ft). The rocket motor was then to have been used intermittently to maintain altitude until its fuel was exhausted, whereupon the DFS 228 would glide back to friendly territory. Depending on thermal conditions, it was confidently expected that the aircraft would be able to return from targets over 1000km (620 miles) away.

Only a few were constructed. Many test flights were made, all of them it is believed (though there are differing reports) without rocket power, and a new pressurised cabin, with the pilot in the prone position, was eventually developed and tried out just days before the war's end. Both the original cabin, in which the pilot sat upright, and the later version, which was very much more effective, were attached to the rest of the airframe by explosive bolts. Set free, the nose cone deployed a parachute and descended with the pilot still on board until the outside temperature and pressure reached life-supporting levels, whereupon his seat or couch was ejected by compressed air and he made a normal parachute descent.

A development of the DFS 228, the DFS 346, was designed as a supersonic trials aircraft. It was to have had two rocket motors, variable-chord swept wings and a Multhopp-style T-tail, but was otherwise similar to the DFS 228 in its later incarnation, although constructed entirely of stressed aluminium rather than wood. An unpowered prototype was to have been built (in wood). It is believed that this aircraft and a number of somewhat modified DFS 346s were constructed in the Soviet Union after the war, and there are persistent but unsubstantiated claims that the former was the first aircraft to exceed the speed of sound with DFS test pilot Wolfgang Ziese at the controls in May 1947, some five months before Chuck Yeager's supersonic flight in a Bell X-1 on 14 October.

THE GIANT TRANSPORT GLIDERS

At the other end of the performance scale, two projects to develop heavy-lift gliders capable of carrying up to 22,000kg (48,500lb) of cargo – the approximate weight of a combat infantry company, with all its equipment – were ordered up by the RLM: one of them from Messerschmitt, as the Me 321 'Gigant' ('Giant'); the other from Junkers, as the Ju 322 'Mammut' ('Mammoth'), originally named 'Goliath'. The Messerschmitt aircraft was ultimately to be the most successful by far, with about 200 built, but the Junkers 'Mammut' was the more interesting of the two, despite being a constructive failure.

THE Me 321 'GIGANT'

The Me 321 was conventional in that it had a fuselage to which the high-set wings and empennage were attached. It was constructed from welded steel tubing and wood with a covering of fabric and wood, and its fuselage was rectangular in cross-section, very tall towards the nose (which had clam-shell doors for loading and unloading vehicles) and tapering towards the tail, with side doors at the rear for passengers. The cockpit was located on top of the fuselage, level with the leading edge of the wing, which was straight and tapered, with a span of 55m (180.5ft), braced by struts to the fuselage floor at the point where the fixed wheels were mounted. The tail was composed of a tall fin and a braced tailplane. The aircraft performed perfectly from the first flight, which took place at Leipheim in March 1941, and was quite capable of lifting the design payload. The first examples entered service in May 1941, when a squadron of 18 was formed. Originally, the 'Giants' were towed either by a trio of Bf 110s (the so-called 'Troika-Schlepp') or

by a single Ju 290, and later by the specially developed He 111Z 'Zwilling' ('Twin'), which was, in effect, two He 111s joined at the wing, outboard of the engines, the junction being effected at a fifth engine, thus giving one outboard of each fuselage, and three in the wing area between them. Rockets of various types were mounted to assist take-off, and there were plans to mount Argus pulse-jets to increase the aircraft's gliding range after release. The principal work of the 'Giant' was to transport material to the Eastern Front. It had a crew of two and was armed with four 7.92mm machine guns.

Even before the prototype glider had taken to the air, work was in hand to transform it into a powered aircraft. This consisted mainly of strengthening its structure and contriving mountings for engines, initially four supercharged Gnome-Rhône 14Ns, which produced around 1150hp each. The prototype flew in April 1942 and since it was considered to be underpowered, the next aircraft had six engines, as did the aircraft of all subsequent productions. The Me 323, as it was designated, was something of a handful in the air, requiring two flight engineers to keep the engines balanced, and two gunners, with a total of five 7.92 mm (later 13mm) machine guns, plus locations for 10 MG34 infantry machine guns in the fuselage sides. It often needed the assistance of a tow-plane or rocket motors to get off the ground, especially when heavily laden. It could carry around 16.25 tonnes (16 tons) of payload, and had seats for 130 passengers (though many more were carried in evacuation operations, for

Below: The heavily laden 'Gigant' – this is an Me 323 – proved sickeningly vulnerable to air-to-air attack. In April 1943, no fewer than 20 were shot down in one operation.

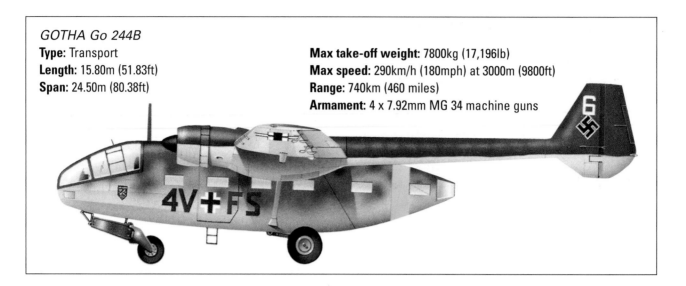

GOTHA Go 244B
Type: Transport
Length: 15.80m (51.83ft)
Span: 24.50m (80.38ft)
Max take-off weight: 7800kg (17,196lb)
Max speed: 290km/h (180mph) at 3000m (9800ft)
Range: 740km (460 miles)
Armament: 4 x 7.92mm MG 34 machine guns

Above: Like the Messerschmitt 'Gigant', the much smaller Gotha Go 242 also made the transition from glider to powered aircraft, becoming the Go 244 in the process.

example). It first became operational in November 1942, and was used to supply units of the Afrika Korps from a base in Sicily. Although it was largely successful, it did have its spectacular failures. On 22 April 1943, no less than 21 Me 323s, ferrying petrol, were shot down in a single operation. Production continued until mid-1944, and around 200 examples were built in all.

THE Ju 322 'MAMMUT'

The heavy glider Junkers produced was anything but conventional. Designed by Heinrich Hertel, it was simply an enormous flying wing, inside which it carried almost all of its payload, with a tall fin carried on a boom-like extension at the tail. In overall form it was somewhat reminiscent of the Junkers-G 38, a commercial passenger-carrier which made its first flight in 1929. On RLM instructions, the Ju 322 was constructed entirely from wood. With a span of 62m (203.5ft) and a length of 30.25m (99.25ft) it had a wing area of 925m² (9952 sq ft). The centre section of the wing's straight leading edge housed a top-hinged loading door, with a glazed cupola to the port side of it containing the flight deck. The upper surface of the wing was flat, and there was considerable dihedral on the lower surface. At the centre point, it was over 3m (9.8ft) thick. The prototype did fly in April 1941 but by that time its payload had been cut to half of the required 22.35 tonnes (22 tons) as the 'cabin' floor was simply not up to the task: a tracked vehicle actually broke through it during loading trials and the air-

craft proved to be chronically unstable. It landed safely and was towed back to the airfield at Merseburg. Given a larger tail fin in an attempt to counter the instability, it made a few more test flights before the project was abandoned on the orders of the RLM. It was then cut up for fuel, along with a completed second aircraft and the components of 98 more which were already in the process of construction.

THE GOTHA Go 242/244

Somewhat more practical than either of the giant gliders and more numerous by far was the Gotha Go 242. It was a shoulder-wing monoplane with a simple square-section fuselage culminating in twin booms linked by a cross-plane to form the tail. A loading ramp at the rear of the fuselage pod let down to allow loading and unloading of a small vehicle such as the amphibious Kübelwagen, or 21 fully equipped troops. Over 1500 were built, of which 133 were converted into Go 244s, fitted with two 700hp Gnome-Rhône engines in forward extensions of the tailbooms.

A few of the gliders were converted to allow them to alight on water; they carried a small catamaran assault boat with a 1200kg (2646lb) explosive charge suspended between its hulls. The mission profile envisaged for them saw the pilot setting down near an enemy ship and taking to the assault boat, setting off in it at high speed toward the ship and locking the controls before baling out to be rescued later by seaplane or submarine. No such mission ever took place, though it is worth remembering that members of the Italian Navy's Xth MAS flotilla disabled the cruiser HMS *York* with explosive-packed motor boats at Suda Bay in Crete in March 1941, so the idea was not that far-fetched.

HYBRID AND COMPOSITE AIRCRAFT

Engineers on both sides during World War II gave considerable thought to the problems associated with guiding unmanned explosives-packed aircraft to a target. We shall see in Chapter Five how the USAAF used remotely controlled B-17s to complete the destruction of V weapons sites in France in 1944, but long before that, in 1940, the RLM had turned the problem over to DFS. The parameters the Institute was given included supporting parasite fighter aircraft and refuelling heavily loaded bombers in flight as well as guiding a flying bomb to its target zone, and the first tentative solution was to tow one aircraft with another using either a flexible cable or a semi-rigid bar which could contain or support a fuel hose. There was a persistent belief that such a system had merit, and experiments with it continued until 1945, but by late 1941, one of the Institute's teams had begun to work on a means of mounting one aircraft on another, piggyback-style, and in January 1942 the 'Mistel' ('Mistletoe') concept received official approval. Soon, Junkers and autopilot-maker Patin were ordered to collaborate with DFS, and within little over a year, work had begun on assembling a prototype combination of Ju 88A-4 and Bf 109F-1.

'MISTEL' 1

DFS's first task had been to devise a suitable structure to co-locate the two aircraft so that the stresses acting on them would be transmitted between the two main spars, with coupling links which could be sundered either mechanically or explosively. The result was a pair of tripod struts, the apex of which hooked into plates on the underside of the Bf 109's wing roots, the two outer bases of each located on load-bearing plates which traversed the main spar, while the inner legs located on to it directly through the fuselage top. A single pole supported the Messerschmitt's tail and kept the fuselage axes parallel. In later combinations, the fighter sat at a 15-degree nose-down angle.

The steering and control system was located in the rear of the Junker's fuselage and consisted of a master compass, a steering compass and a three-axis autopilot from Patin. This apparatus was used to steer the combination in normal flight via servos and two simple thumb switches in the fighter's cockpit, one for rudder and ailerons, the other for elevators, with the fighter's controls remaining free. However, the two aircraft's control systems could be linked, and thus operated from the fighter by the usual combination of stick and pedals (via servos, once again), at will. Either the bomber's two engines alone, or all three, could be used, depending on the speed and range required, all fuel being supplied from the host aircraft. This was by no means the only modification needed to the bomber component – in fact, the aircraft were virtually gutted and rebuilt – but the amount of work needed on the fighter was minimal. In order to accommodate the explosive 'warhead', the existing Ju 88 nose section, including the glazed cupola which formed the cockpit cover, was removed entirely, and a solid bulkhead built up. The 3500kg (7720lb) hollow charge, with its distinctive proboscis-like extension

Below: One of the earliest 'Mistel' combinations (they were known unofficially as 'Vater und Sohn' – father and son) matched the Messerschmitt Bf 109F with the Junkers Ju 88A-4. Testing began in July 1943.

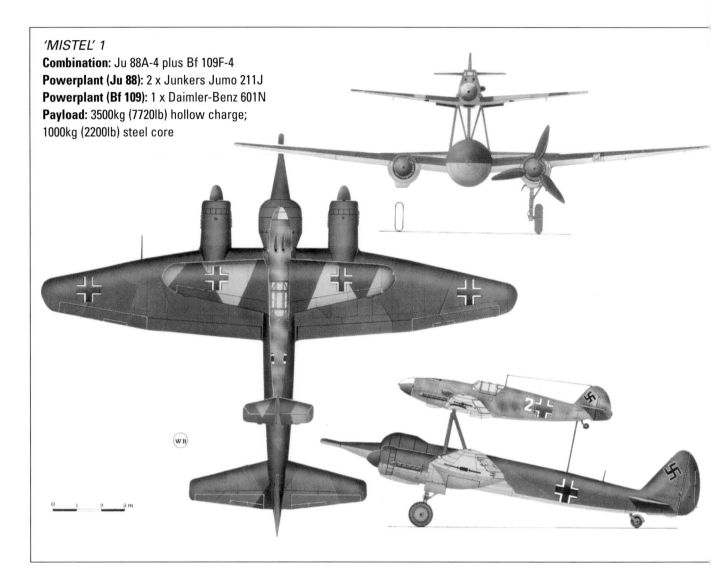

'MISTEL' 1
Combination: Ju 88A-4 plus Bf 109F-4
Powerplant (Ju 88): 2 x Junkers Jumo 211J
Powerplant (Bf 109): 1 x Daimler-Benz 601N
Payload: 3500kg (7720lb) hollow charge;
1000kg (2200lb) steel core

Above: The operational 'Mistel' (this page) paired a fighter with a bomber whose nose was replaced with a warhead. Trainers (facing page) retained the standard nose.

and 1000kg (2200lb) steel core, could then be mounted on the bulkhead; for training missions, a standard two-man nose section, stripped of all non-essentials, could be mounted in its place. Operationally, the procedure of launching the bomber component was straightforward. The pilot lined the combination up with the target in a shallow dive using his standard reflecting gunsight, activated the automatic pilot, and then broke free. Some elected to attempt to suppress local flak before setting out to return to their base.

'MISTEL' TARGETS REVEALED

The first flight of the combination took place in July 1943, and the testing procedure was successfully completed by October, by which time development

work on the warhead was well advanced and 15 combinations had been ordered from Junkers, who were responsible for the conversion itself. By April 1944, a small unit, designated 2/KG101, and under the command of Hauptmann Horst Rudat, had been set up and had begun training, initially at the Junkers airfield at Norhausen, later at Kolberg on the Baltic coast. In mid-month, a staff paper outlined the targets for the unit (initially with just five pilots) as shipping in Scapa Flow, Gibraltar Roads and Leningrad, though the latter two were soon rejected as being impractically far away. Scapa Flow was chosen as the first objective, and the aircraft were to take off from Grove in Denmark and cross the North Sea following a line of pre-positioned radio buoys. Planning had reached a fairly advanced stage when the Allies landed in Normandy, and in mid-June, 2/KG101 moved to St Dizier, from where five 'Mistels' took off just after dark on 24 June to attack shipping in the Baie de la

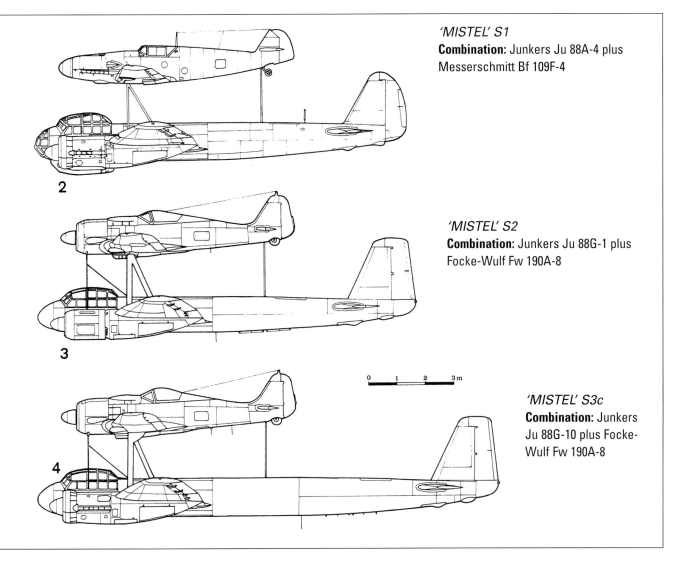

'MISTEL' S1
Combination: Junkers Ju 88A-4 plus Messerschmitt Bf 109F-4

'MISTEL' S2
Combination: Junkers Ju 88G-1 plus Focke-Wulf Fw 190A-8

'MISTEL' S3c
Combination: Junkers Ju 88G-10 plus Focke-Wulf Fw 190A-8

Seine. Four of the five aircraft involved were reported to have hit shipping targets, the fifth pilot jettisoning his host bomber after a mechanical failure.

Over the course of the next four months, more units were trained in the operation of the combination and two more 'Mistel' raids took place, one on shipping in the English Channel, the other on Scapa Flow. Neither was successful. In the course of the latter, three aircraft crashed and the other two failed to find the target. By now, other combinations had been ordered which paired more recent models of the Ju 88 with Fw 190s, and the factory at Bernberg was producing them from new – not re-cycled – aircraft. Attention turned east in November 1944, and training for Operation 'Eisenhammer' commenced, which was a campaign aimed at destroying electrical power stations in the Soviet Union. As the Allied armies closed in on the Reich from east and west, bridges in particular became important targets, and through the spring

of 1945, it was against river crossings and bridgeheads that the 'Misteln' were used exclusively. The last operation took place on 16 April 1945.

Many other combinations of aircraft types were projected (and in some cases built) for use in 'Mistel' operations, including Dornier Do 217K/DFS 228, for reconnaissance, the host aircraft acting as a mobile, high-altitude launch pad; Do 217/Fw 190, for pathfinder missions, the fighter protecting the host aircraft; and Ta 154/Fw 190, Me 262/Me 262, Ju 287/Me 262 and Ju 268/He 162 combinations, all of which were proposed for use against high-value targets, where approach speed might have been thought to make a significant difference. By 1945, DFS was working on remote-control systems using both the radio link and the television guidance system specially devised for the Hs 293 guided bomb (see Chapter Seven). A test aircraft had been prepared, but it was destroyed by fire before trials could begin.

Rotary-wing Aircraft

Rotary-wing aircraft were first demonstrated as early as 1907, but it was 1936 before a satisfactory design for a helicopter was developed, in Germany. The Reich's scientists took the lead in this field, and by 1945 had developed operational rotary-wing craft and demonstrated just how effective they could be in combat conditions.

Above: The Flettner Fl 282 'Kolibri' was a fully operational helicopter despite its somewhat rudimentary appearance.

Left: 'Dare anything' test pilot Hanna Reitsch shows off the Focke Achgelis Fa 61 inside Berlin's *Deutschlandhalle*.

Rotary-wing aircraft can be divided into two basic types: autogiros and helicopters. Autogiros, such as that devised by Juan de la Cierva, derive their lift from their forward momentum, which is supplied by a conventionally positioned propeller, and their rotors are unpowered. They can take off only with a run, they cannot fly except in the forwards direction, and

they cannot hover, but they can descend and land almost vertically. Cierva made the first successful flight in an autogiro in January 1923, having found that it was necessary to articulate the blades where they joined the hub. For some years, autogiros seemed set to overshadow true helicopters, examples of which had been flying since 1907, but once Cierva's articulated rotor head arrangement was adopted, the latter surged to the fore once more, although work on autogiros continued, too. By the late 1930s, Germany had become the centre of helicopter development; in the period up to May 1945, almost 20 rotary-wings of different types were designed there, including autogiros,

Above: The Fa 223 'Drache' ('Kite') was the first truly viable transport helicopter. This example was constructed in Czechoslovakia after the war, from salvaged parts.

girogliders and manned kites. The only work of any note undertaken elsewhere was that of the Russian emigré Igor Sikorsky in the United States. Sikorsky made his first experiments with rotary-wing flight in 1909, but did not achieve comparative success until 30 years later, though he was to become crucial to the type's development.

THE FOCKE ACHGELIS Fa 61

In the early 1930s, Professor Heinrich Karl Focke began building Cierva C.19 autogiros under licence in Germany – and separately from his partnership with Georg Wulf – and soon began experimenting with helicopters. Focke collaborated with Gerd Achgelis, who flew a Kurt Tank-designed Fw 44 'Steiglitz' ('Goldfinch') in aerobatics displays (as did Ernst Udet), and soon produced a design for a twin-rotor helicopter, the Fa 61. This resembled the Cierva machine in that it was composed of a conventional fuselage with a front-mounted radial engine (a BMW Bramo Sh 14, of 160hp), but differed in having two outrigger-mounted three-bladed rotors, driven by shafts in contra-rotation to neutralise torque effect. There was a small conventionally placed propeller, but only to assist engine cooling. The tail had a fin and rudder and top-mounted stabilisers, and the craft sat on a tail-wheel undercarriage but with a nose wheel to prevent it from nosing over. The rotors had cyclic pitch control (that is, the angle of attack of the individual blades was varied during the rotation cycle) which gave longitudinal and directional control, and differential operation of the two cyclics gave

lateral control by inducing asymmetric lift. The Fa 61 made its maiden flight in the hands of Ewald Rohlfs on 26 June 1936, lasting 28 seconds. But by the following year, Rohlfs was setting and breaking records regularly. On the anniversary of the maiden flight, he established a height record of 2440m (8000ft) and an endurance record of 1hr:20min:49sec. The following day he set straight-line and curcuit distance records and a speed record of 122.553km/h (76.1mph) over a 20km (12.5 mile) course. Hanna Reitsch broke the straight-line record with a flight of almost 109km (67.7 miles) between Bremen and Berlin four months later, and in February the following year, she actually flew the helicopter inside the *Deutschlandhalle* in Berlin to demonstrate its controllability. On 29 January 1929, Karl Bode established a height record which was to remain unbroken for some time when he took the machine to 3427m (11,240.5ft).

The Fa 61 was hardly a secret weapon. Indeed, it was developed very publicly and was really little more than a concept demonstrator, but there was much better to come both from Focke Achgelis and from a competitor, Anton Flettner, during the course of the war. The Wehrmacht was quick to appreciate the operational possibilities the type opened up. In 1938 Focke Achgelis began work on a genuine transport helicopter known originally as the Fa 266 'Hornisse' ('Hornet'), and later as the Fa 223

'Drache' ('Kite'). The new aircraft was essentially an enlarged version of the Fa 61, with the same boomed-out twin-rotor layout, but it was much more powerful, with a supercharged 650hp Bramo 323 Q3 'Fafnir' engine, and more flexible and easier to fly, thanks to the introduction of collective pitch control. Previously, ascent had been controlled by the throttle, a very hit-and-miss affair; with the introduction of collective pitch control, the degree of lift was controlled by adjusting the pitch of the rotor blades, and engine speed stayed constant. The fuselage, 12.25m (40ft) long, was fabricated from steel tubes and covered with fabric except on the engine compartment, where sheet metal was used. It was divided into four compartments: the cockpit, with seats for pilot and observer; the load compartment, with a starboard-side door, where self-sealing fuel and oil tanks were also located; the engine compartment; and the tail section, which was a conventional fin and rudder with a top-mounted stabiliser, adjustable for trim.

UNUSUAL ENGINE MOUNTING

The method of mounting the engine was somewhat bizarre. Both it and the gearbox were located in two large-diameter rings, which were attached to four longitudinal fuselage members by adjustable cables, with struts to prevent fore-and-aft movement. There was a gap in the fuselage covering at the forward end of the engine compartment, through which cooling air entered, and another at its after end, whence it escaped. The rotor blades were made from wooden ribs attached to a high-tensile steel tube, and covered with plywood and fabric. The rotor discs were inclined inwards by 4.5 degrees, and slightly forwards, and normal speed of rotation was 275rpm, a 9.1:1 reduction from engine speed.

The 'Drache' (it was also known as the 'Draken': 'Dragon') could carry up to four passengers in the load compartment but during troop manoeuvres in 1944, it carried 12 fully equipped soldiers, the other eight travelling outside on tractor seats on the outriggers. Its total payload capacity was around 1.27 tonnes (1.25 tons). A Fieseler 'Storch' aircraft and a Volkswagen car were lifted in demonstrations, and small field pieces were transported during army manoeuvres; large loads were slung from a winch on a load-bearing beam via a port in the aircraft's floor.

The Fa 266 prototype was completed at the end of 1939 and, by now redesignated as the Fa 223, made its first free flight in August 1940 after more than 100 hours of static and tethered hovering trials. Karl Bode

flew it to the RLM test centre at Rechlin in October 1940, and set a batch of new records: a speed of 182km/h (113mph); a vertical rate of climb of 528m (1732ft) per minute; and an altitude of 7252m (23,295ft) where normal operational limits were 120km/h (74.5mph) and 4880m (16,010ft). The RLM promptly ordered 30 for evaluation in the anti-submarine, reconnaissance, rescue, training, and transport roles and it was decided before series production commenced to build standardised aircraft which would be equipped according to the requirements of their mission.

The first prototype, -V1, was wrecked on 5 February 1941 after having made 115 flights, when a power failure occurred while it was in a low hover. In June 1942, the second and third prototypes, along with seven pre-production machines and much of the tooling, were destroyed in an air raid. Production was then moved from Bremen to Laupheim in southern Germany but did not restart until February 1943. More aircraft were destroyed when the new factory was bombed in its turn, in July 1944, and as a result, the number of Fa 223s completed was probably no more than 12. Three were still in operational service at the end of the war; one was destroyed by its pilot and two were seized by the Americans. One of them was subsequently flown to England by Helmut Gersenhauer, the Luftwaffe's most experienced helicopter pilot, and was flown for around 170 hours in trials before crashing from a height of 18.3m (60ft). After the war, development of the Fa 223 continued in France (with Professor Focke's assistance) and in Czechoslovakia, where two were constructed from salvaged parts. That the Fa 223 was not more widely produced, when all concerned agreed that it was a useful addition to the Luftwaffe's catalogue of aircraft, is understandable only within the terms of the struggle for the allocation of resources going on within the Third Reich at the time. Clearly, it had no champion sufficiently powerful to push it high enough up the list of priorities. Had -V12 not broken down when transporting the captured Italian dictator, Benito Mussolini, from the hotel on the Gran Sasso in September 1943 when he was rescued by Otto Skorzeny, perhaps things might have been different!

THE Fa 225

The Luftwaffe's interest in gliders dated back to the time before Germany was permitted an air force, when the only means she had of training pilots was to set up gliding clubs and schools. As well as acting as

Above: The Fa 330 was not a true helicopter but an unpowered girokite; it was designed to be towed behind a submarine as an observation platform.

a valuable means of instructing personnel, gliders were to become important in themselves in a number of roles. The first operational use of a glider to transport troops and equipment directly into combat occurred on 10 May 1940, when Luftwaffe paratroops siezed and held the Belgian frontier fortress of Eben-Emael after landing on it in DFS 230 gliders. This was to be the most effective type in German service during World War II, but it could be employed only where there was a suitable, fairly large, landing site. Focke Achgelis suggested improving on this by substituting a three-bladed rotor unit from an Fa 223 for the wings of a DFS 230, producing what was in effect an externally powered autogiro or giroglider, which, when cast loose, would simply autorotate to the ground at a very steep angle of approach, and would thus be able to land in an area not much larger than itself. It was to be towed behind the Luftwaffe's maid-of-all-work, the Ju 52, and in tests carried out during 1943, it was found to be practicable to land it and come to a halt within 18.3m (60ft). Though the Fa 225, as the hybrid glider was known, worked well enough, by the time it was ready to go into production, the Wehrmacht's operational requirements had changed and the project was shelved.

THE Fa 330 'BACHSTELZE'

The Fa 225 was not the only unpowered rotary-wing aircraft Focke Achgelis was to design. Early in 1942, the company was asked to devise a simple single-seat girokite to be towed behind a submarine, from which an observer would be able to monitor a much wider area than would a look-out stationed on the boat itself. The result, the Fa 330 'Bachstelze' ('Water Wagtail'), was simple in the extreme: two steel tubes, the shorter, which supported the rotor assembly, being set at right-angles to the longer, which held the simple rudder assembly and the pilot's seat and rudimentary controls, by means of which he could tilt the rotor head (which gave longitudinal and lateral control) and turn the rudder to change direction. The pitch of the rotor blades could be adjusted, but not in flight. Coarse pitch gave the best flying performance, but made launching rather more difficult. The Fa 330 was launched by setting the rotor turning (by hand if there was a wind; by means of a rope wound around a drum in the rotor head if there was not) and then pushing the whole machine backwards. Recovery was by means of a winch under normal circumstances, but in an emergency, the pilot could release the rotor, which deployed a parachute from its stowage behind the pilot's seat as it flew off. The winch held 150m (492ft) of towing cable, which permitted the kite to fly at an altitude of 120m (395ft); from there, the horizon was 40km (25 miles) away, a marked improvement over the 8km (5 miles) horizon from the boat itself. Without its pilot, the girokite weighed 82kg (180lb), and could be assembled and dismantled in a matter of minutes. Minimum speed required to stay aloft was 27km/h (17mph).

Something like 200 Fa 330s were produced by Weser-Flugzeugbau and were deployed aboard Type IX ocean-going U-boats, but little is known about their operational history beyond the fact that two or three crewmembers from each boat were taught how to fly them in the wind tunnel at Chalais-Meudon near Paris. They were said to be very easy indeed to operate, and would fly quite happily hands-off for short periods, but were unpopular with their pilots for reasons of self-preservation.

AMBITIOUS FOCKE DESIGNS

Focke Achgelis also produced two very much more ambitious designs, one of them, the Fa 269, for a convertiplane, which would have landed and taken off vertically but then turned the shaft carrying the rotors through 90 degrees to bring them to the position of pusher propellers. Such an arrangement (but employing more efficient tractor propellers) was not to be successfully introduced until Boeing-Vertol perfected the V-22 Osprey in the late 1980s. The Fa 269 was really little more than a flight of fancy, and it is to be doubted if the technology of the day could actually have realised it. The Fa 284 was much more practical, being, in effect, a stretched version of the Fa 223, with a fuselage which was largely of lattice construction and twin 1600hp BMW 801 engines. It was designed to carry heavy loads underslung, in exactly the same way as its 1970s equivalent, the Sikorsky S-60 (CH-54B) 'Flying Crane', did. Some parts are said to have been manufactured before the project was cancelled in late 1943 and plans were drawn up to produce a twin Fa 223, essentially two aircraft joined, in-line, by a short fuselage section. This section is known to have been produced, but the complete aircraft was not.

By far the most adventurous of Professor Focke's designs was presented under the auspices of Focke-Wulf rather than Focke Achgelis. Known as the 'Triebflügel' ('Thrustwing'), this was a tail-sitting VTOL (Vertical Take-Off and Landing) aircraft which derived its lift from three wings which rotated around the fuselage just aft of the cockpit, under the power of tip-mounted ramjets giving about 840kg (1850lb) of thrust, the wings being brought up to operating speed by three jettisonable rockets. In flight, the wings would be rotated around their individual axes until

they became conventional aerofoils as the aircraft itself rotated until its axis was horizontal rather than vertical. No real development work was ever done on the concept, and the viability of the design is a matter of speculation, but three tail-sitting VTOL aircraft were built post-war, two in the USA and one in France. The American designs, from Lockheed and Convair, were somewhat more conventional, in that they used fixed wings and contra-rotating propellers in the nose, while the French SNECMA 'Coleopter' was powered by a tail-mounted turbojet and had an annular wing, control being achieved through four swivelling fins. All three aircraft flew after a fashion, but all projects were eventually cancelled. The objective has since been achieved by vectoring the thrust of a turbojet in a more-or-less conventional airframe.

ANTON FLETTNER

Having turned his attention to the problems of rotary-wing flight in 1930, Anton Flettner first produced a helicopter with two 30hp Anzani piston engines mounted on the ends of two rotors, each turning a two-bladed propeller. While this arrangement eliminated the problems associated with torque (which the Focke Achgelis designs overcame by means of two contrarotating rotor sets, and which other designers,

Below: The Fl 282 was the most sophisticated of all German helicopters of World War II. This later version – captured by US forces – even had protection for the pilot.

notably Sikorsky, counteracted by means of a powered tail rotor), it was only marginally successful in other ways. When it was destroyed during tethered testing, it was not rebuilt. Flettner next built a two-seat cabin autogiro for the *Kriegsmarine* (German Navy) but the single example of the Fl 184 caught fire in flight and was also destroyed.

THE FI 185 AND FI 265

Clearly, Anton Flettner was still searching for a valid way forward, for his next design, designated the Fl 185, was substantially different again, almost a cross between a helicopter and an autogiro, its 140hp Siemens-Halke engine being linked to a single rotor and two variable-pitch pusher propellers located on outriggers. For vertical take-off and landing, the aircraft functioned as a helicopter, the majority of the power going to the rotor, and the two conventional propellers, providing thrust in opposite directions, only counteracting the torque. For forward flight, the rotor autorotated and the two propellers received all the power and gave forward thrust. The Fl 185 flew only a few times before Flettner abandoned it and turned his attention to a new design using synchronised intermeshing contra-rotating twin rotors (like those of the Kaman H-43 'Huskie' of the 1960s) with differential collective pitch control.

The single-seat Fl 265 was very similar in appearance to the Fl 185, with its front-mounted radial engine with cowl and cooling fan, enclosed cockpit

Below: The Fl 282 was ordered in 1944 after sea trials aboard the cruiser *Köln* had shown it could be flown even in adverse conditions. Only Allied bombing prevented the aircraft going into service.

and stubby tailfin. However, gone were the Fl 185's outriggers and propellers, and the rotor head assembly, with its paired, inclined shafts, each with a two-bladed rotor, was much more complex. The design was completed in 1937, and the following year, the *Kriegsmarine* ordered six aircraft for evaluation purposes. The prototype made its maiden flight in May 1939, and was later destroyed when its rotor blades struck each other in flight.

Other Fl 265s were used extensively for operational trials with naval units – cruisers in the main, but also submarines – in the Baltic and the Mediterranean with considerable success, and completely validated the concept of deploying VTOL aircraft with warships. Aircraft also operated with army units, both in the reconnaissance and logistical roles, and a Luftwaffe trial involving a Bf 109 and an Fw 190 fitted with camera guns demonstrated that the helicopter was very difficult to shoot down. The two fighters, amongst the best in the world, we may recall, attacked the Fl 265 for 20 minutes but failed to score a single hit. The outcome of the various trials was that Flettner was ordered to proceed with volume production. In fact, he had already proceeded with the design of an updated version, the two-seat (some prototypes were single-seat) Fl 282 'Kolibri' ('Hummingbird'), and it was this aircraft which went into manufacture.

THE FI 282 'KOLIBRI'

The most important modification Flettner made to the design of the new aircraft was to re-locate the engine behind the pilot's seat, which gave him and the observer a much-enlarged field of view. The drive was taken off the front of the crankshaft through a reduction gearbox and transmitted up and back through a

FLETTNER FI 282 V21
Type: Single-seat open-cockpit helicopter
Length: 6.56m (21.52ft)
Max take-off weight: 1000kg (2200lb)
Max speed: 150km/h (93mph) at sea level
Range: 170km (106 miles)
Ceiling: 3290m (10,800ft)
Armament: None

universally jointed drive shaft and a cross-shaft connecting the two rotor shafts, which were set at an inclusive angle of 24 degrees, and inclined forward by 6 degrees. The rotor blades were mounted so that they were parallel when they were at 45 degrees to the aircraft's centreline. The fin and rudder were much larger than in previous Flettner designs, steering being accomplished by a combination of rudder movement and differential collective pitch control.

The 'Kolibri' proved to be very satisfactory indeed, despite a pronounced vibration period as the engine was run-up, with a maximum speed in level flight of 150km/h (93mph), a vertical rate of climb of 91.5m/min (300ft/min), a hover ceiling of 300m (985ft), and a service ceiling of 3290m (10,800ft). Its range, with just the pilot and maximum fuel aboard, was 300km (185 miles). Some 50 pilots were trained to fly it, most of them by Flettner's test pilot, Hans Fuisting. It was extremely manoeuvrable and very stable and at forward speeds in excess of 60km/h (37mph) could be flown hands-off once the controls were balanced.

SEA TRIALS

From 1942, trials at sea aboard the cruiser *Köln* demonstrated that the aircraft was usable even in very poor weather conditions, and by the following year, 20 were in service with the *Kriegsmarine* in the Mediterranean and the Aegean. In 1944, an order for 1000 Fl 282s was placed with BMW, which began tooling up for production at its Munich and Eisenach plants, but before manufacture could begin, both they

Above: An American airman examines the tiny rotor-tip jets which Friedrich von Doblhoff proposed to use to eliminate the effects of engine torque in his WNF 342.

and the Flettner works at Johannisthal were very badly damaged by Allied bombing. Anton Flettner went on to design a 20-seat passenger helicopter, the Fl 339, but never got beyond the development stage.

THE DOBLHOFF/WNF 342

Friedrich von Doblhoff is rather less well-known than the other helicopter pioneers in the Third Reich, but the machines which he designed, and which were built by Wiener Neustadter Flugzeugwerke in the Vienna suburbs, represented yet another innovatory approach to the solution of the torque problem. Doblhoff used small rotor-tip jets to drive the blades. A combustible air/fuel mixture was fed to small combustion chambers in the rotor tips using a compressor driven by a conventional piston engine. The mixture travelled by way of the rotor hub and passages in the rotors themselves, before being ignited. The piston engine also drove a small fan which blew air over the tail surfaces for the purpose of steering. Only four prototypes were built; the first three had fixed-pitch blades, and were only ever used in static/tethered tests, but the fourth had a most ingenious (and very complex) arrangement which allowed collective pitch control. The last prototype was behaving well in its trials and had been flown at speeds of up to 45km/h (28mph) when the programme was halted by the arrival of Soviet forces in 1945.

Surface-to-Surface Missiles

Until the outbreak of World War II, rocketry was hardly a science at all; until then it had consisted of really nothing more than a few scattered and sporadic attempts to shoot small projectiles straight up into the sky, virtually for the sake of it. All that changed when it became clear that the rocket had potential as a long-range weapon of war, and nowhere was this potential better understood than in Germany, where much of the pioneering work on rockets had been done anyway.

Most famous of the German secret weapons of World War II – and by far the most effective – were the surface-to-surface missiles used to bombard the United Kingdom and targets on the mainland of Europe, particularly the port of Antwerp, from late June 1944. As well as the so-called 'Vengeance Weapons', the V1 and V2, there were other types (though only one was operational, and then only in a

Above: The Fi 103 R – the manned V1.

Left: This A4 – or V2 – was captured by British forces and fired by British scientists near Cuxhaven in 1945.

very limited sense), designed to supply data on flight characteristics and to act as concept vehicles for operational types. Not surprisingly, given the success of the V2 ballistic missile, there were plans to develop it still further, though none passed the prototype stage, and most existed only on paper. Many of the scientists and engineers who worked on Germany's rocketry programme went on after the war to become prime movers in the rocketry and space exploration programmes of both the United States of America and the Soviet Union, and were thus instrumental in both putting man into space and establishing a technology which has become a mainstay of modern civilisation.

THE FIESELER Fi 103 – THE V1

The Vergeltungswaffe 1 (the revenge, or retaliation, weapon), or V1, had a plethora of names. To the Luftwaffe, it was the Fliegerabwehrkanonezielgerät 76 (Flakzielgerät 76, or just FZG 76), but that was a cover-name: *Fliegerabwehrkanonezielgerät* means 'anti-aircraft gun aiming device' or conceivably 'anti-aircraft gun target device'. Its official codename was 'Kirschkern' ('Cherrystone') and it was also known as 'Krähe' ('Crow'); while to the RLM it was the Fi 103; and to the airframe manufacturers, Fieseler, it began life as P. 35. To the British public it was the Buzzbomb, the P-Plane or the Doodlebug, while the RAF knew it as 'Diver'. In effect a first-generation cruise missile, it was an unmanned air-breathing jet aircraft with an explosive warhead and a simple guidance/targeting device, and to relate its history from the very start, we need to go back to 1928.

Paul Schmidt worked primarily in the associated fields of fluid dynamics and aerodynamics, but in 1928 he began experimenting with a simple form of thrust engine known as a pulse-jet. In essence, a pulse-jet is a tubular combustion chamber with a matrix of small, rectangular, spring-loaded flap-valves at the front, into which a suitable fuel (it need be no more exotic than petrol, and low-octane petrol, at that) is injected. The device must be accelerated by

Above: The infamous V1 self-propelled guided bomb. The proto-cruise missile carried a warhead of 830kg (1832lb) of amatol to targets up to about 240km (150 miles) away.

Below: The Argus pulse-jet – small flaps in the aperture were forced open against a spring by air pressure and forced shut by fuel exploding in the jet pipe behind.

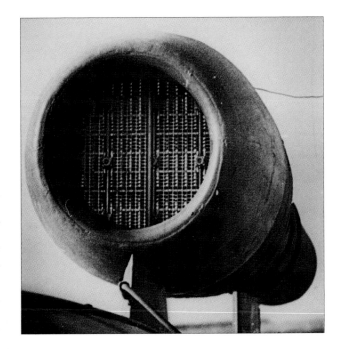

some external means to a critical threshold velocity, something of the order of 300km/h (186mph), before it will work, though there is the option to supply it with air under sufficient pressure and in sufficient quantity by means of a blower system. As the device travels forward, air is forced past the flap-valves and into the tube; the act of opening the flap-valves opens a second valve, which admits a quantity of petrol under pressure into the tube to form an explosive mixture (in exactly the same way that a petrol engine's fuel injection system does), and also activates a sparking plug. The primary result of the explosion is to blow shut the flap-valves, closing off both air flow and petrol flow, and this has the secondary effect of turning aimless explosion into directed thrust. As the pressure within the tube is reduced to below that of the air trying to rush into the engine from the front, the flap-valves are forced open again, and the whole process is repeated, and so on, many times per second; for example, the Argus 109-014 engine used in the operational V1s cycled 47 times per second.

CHEAP AND SIMPLE

In addition to its inability to self-start, the pulse-jet motor has other limiting factors: it works less effectively as the ambient air pressure drops, and functions poorly at much above 3000m (9800 feet); it operates at a fixed speed, though the dimensions of the combustion chamber can be varied to modify it; and the flap-valves are liable to burn out after a relatively short time. But it has several things in its favour, too: firstly, it works; secondly, it is simple to manufacture; and thirdly, it costs very little.

All in all, it was just the thing to power a short-range surface-to-surface missile, and this was one of the uses Schmidt suggested for it after failing to interest anyone in a vertical take-off aircraft powered by it. He submitted a design to the RLM in 1934. Initially it was poorly received, but after a number of rather more eminent scientists, including Wernher von Braun, took up Schmidt's case, both the RLM and the *Heereswaffenamt* (HWA – the German Army's weapons development and procurement office) took more notice. At last Schmidt got development funds, even if not in great amounts. By 1940, Schmidt's pulse-jets were giving over 500kg (1100lb) of static thrust, but the RLM had started to look elsewhere for alternative developers. It looked, in fact, to the rather more prestigious Argus Motoren-Gesellschaft, where Dr Fritz Gosslau and his team began to develop a pulse-jet engine from first principles. They were not

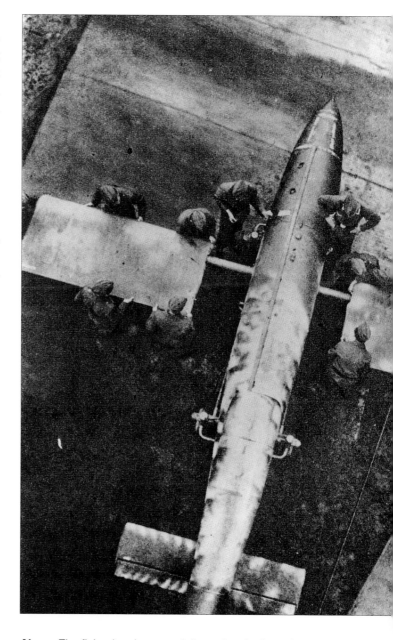

Above: The flying bombs were delivered to the launch sites dismantled, but it was a simple process to assemble them. Here the V1's wings are being introduced over the tubular main spar.

permitted to see Schmidt's engine until March 1940; they adopted his valve system in part, but mostly stuck with their own design. By the end of the year, they had produced a small engine of 150kg (330lb) static thrust, and on 30 April 1941 this engine made its first flight, beneath a Gotha Go 145 two-seater biplane trainer. During the summer, small cargo gliders made flights under pulse-jet power alone, which validated the concept, but it was a further year before the RLM took the next step, and on 19 June 1942,

Above: V1s were launched on ramps by steam catapults. When they reached around 400km/h (250mph), their own powerplants took over and the guidance system took them in a gentle climb to their cruising altitude.

ordered Gerhard Fieseler to begin developing an airframe for a flying bomb. In the meantime Argus carried on developing the powerplant, Walter began work on a catapult launching system, and Siemens set out to produce a guidance system using an existing autopilot as a basis.

The airframe was actually the work of Robert Lusser who, we may recall, was involved in the original P. 1065 project at Messerschmitt, and Willy Fiedler. Development took 18 months, and it was early December of 1942 before the first (unpowered) example was launched from an Fw 200 'Condor' over the test range at Peenemünde-West, to be followed by the first catapult launch on Christmas Eve. In one form or another, a total of perhaps 350 missiles were expended in the course of testing. At the start, testing did not proceed smoothly. The situation was complicated by the necessity to test all the components together, which made fault isolation difficult, but

eventually the design of the air intake and the fuel-supply system were identified as the seats of the worst problems, and when they were re-thought, the bomb flew much more reliably. However, it flew considerably more slowly than had been envisioned, at around 600km/h (370mph), which made it vulnerable to interception by existing fighter aircraft. Consequently, there was a non-stop programme to improve the V1's performance, both by upping the output of the Argus 109-014 motor (by injecting nitrous oxide into the combustion chamber, for example) and by replacing it with a more powerful unit such as the 109-044 or the Porsche 109-005 turbojet – both of which produced 500kg (1100lb) of static thrust – or by an unspecified ramjet. By the war's end, experimental models were flying at almost 800km/h (500mph). By then, they were faced with much faster interceptors, such as the jet-powered Gloster 'Meteor' which scored its first combat victory on 4 August 1944 when it destroyed a V1 by tipping it over with its wingtip to destabilise it. This was not as risky a manoeuvre as one might think, and was deemed preferable to shooting the flying bombs down at close range, with the attendant risk of damage to one's own aircraft. In fact, the V1s were a much easier target for guns on the ground than they were for aircraft, since they flew straight and level and at a fixed speed; more were destroyed by this means than by any other.

DESIGN MODIFICATIONS

Not entirely surprisingly, the guidance system and its installation proved to be problematic, too. The first difficulty actually showed up before the Fi 103 airframe was completed, and involved the positioning of the engine vis-à-vis the fuselage. Tests carried out with engines mounted on Do 17 and Ju 88 aircraft showed that the pulse action produced considerable vibration, particularly if the exhaust stream passed over the fuselage, and so the design was modified to move the entire engine aft so that it overhung the tail by some considerable extent. Close attention had to be paid to the mountings, and eventually a system was adopted which combined a pivoted yoke at the front secured with a single pinned lug to the tail fin, both of the mountings in rubber bushes. However, there were still problems with vibration. The guidance system itself relied on a gyroscope for control in all three axes, linked to a master compass set to the desired heading before launch for azimuth control, and an aneroid barometer for altitude control. Corrections were transmitted to the servo-motors acting on the rudder and elevators by means of compressed air. The distance flown was computed by means of an air-log driven by a small airscrew in the nosecone, and when a predetermined figure had been reached, a pair of detonators exploded, locking the elevator and rudder and deploying two spoilers, forcing the aircraft into a dive. This somewhat complicated procedure was necessary because the temperature in the jet pipe was high enough, even after just a few seconds' running, to sustain ignition alone, as there was no critical timing to worry about, and so the rather simpler method of cutting the current to the spark plug would have had no effect. It would perhaps have been possible to cut the fuel supply instead, though since the fuel system was pressurised this was not entirely predictable

either, and in any event, it was actually more desirable for the vehicle to go into a powered dive. For some time the fuel did tend to cut out as the V1 tipped over. This was not a feature, but a fault which was eventually corrected.

The bomb was equipped with three different types of fuze: an electrical impact fuze, powered by an on-board battery and with a resistor/condenser circuit which held enough charge to detonate the device if the battery connection was severed on impact; an

Below: Since V1s flew at a constant speed, at constant height and on a straight course, it was relatively simple for anti-aircraft gunners to establish a box barrage, particularly at night when the jet flare was obvious.

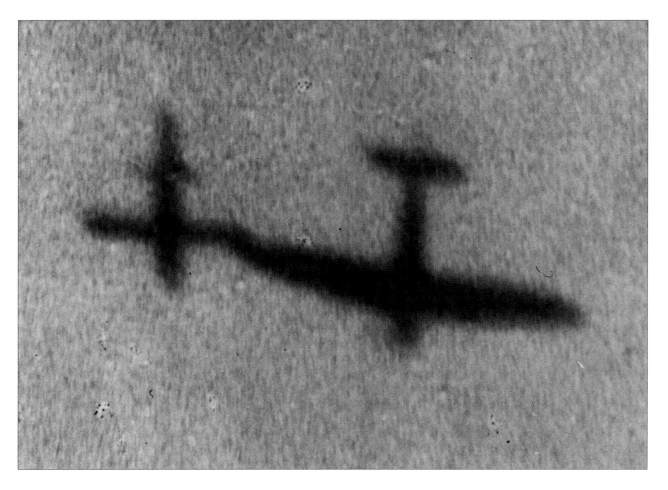

Above: The preferred way to destroy the bombs from the air was to tip them off course – not as risky a business as one might suppose. The aircraft pictured in this gun camera shot is, from its wingform, a Spitfire.

electro-mechanical all-ways fuze with a trembler switch; and a mechanical (clockwork) delayed fuze. The impact fuze had three actuators: one in the nose and one in the belly (both of which functioned by pressure); and an inertial switch in the fuze itself. The fuzing system was so good that of the first 2500 to hit the UK, only four failed to go off.

The launch system was less problematical than other elements, and employed a simple steam catapult, the steam being generated by the reaction of the same T-Stoff and Z-Stoff (basically hydrogen peroxide and calcium or potassium permanganate, as we might recall) used in rocket motors. The catapult track was a slotted tube 42m (138ft) long, inclined at an angle of six and a half degrees (later, a track half that length was employed), on a concrete and steel bed, within which a dumbell-shaped free piston ran. The piston incorporated a fin which protruded through the slot in the tube, and engaged with a simple trolley on which the missile sat. The slot was sealed by a tubular strip which trailed behind the piston to be forced into the slot by the pressure of the steam. The fuel to generate the steam was contained in tanks on a trolley, which also held the forged steel steam generation chamber, secured to the rear of the launch tube by a bayonet fitting. Alongside the rear of the ramp, there was a starter unit which contained the equipment necessary to get the pulse-jet operating.

LAUNCHING THE V1

The launch procedure was straightforward. The pulse jet was fired up and allowed to run for seven seconds, bringing it up to the correct operating temperature. The valve on a large bottle of compressed air was then opened by remote control, forcing 60 litres (13.2 gallons) of T-Stoff and 5 litres (1.09 gallons) of Z-Stoff into the steam generation vessel. Their reaction generated a large volume of super-heated steam, and as soon as the pressure in the chamber built up sufficiently, a restraining bolt sheared, whereupon the piston was free to travel up the tube, carrying launch trolley and missile with it. By the time it reached the end of the track – little more than half a second later, having been accelerated at a rate of around 16 *g* – the whole assembly was travelling at around 400km/h (250mph) and the pulse-jet had started to run independently. The piston was literally fired out of the tube and fell to earth some distance away (along with the launch trolley) to be recovered later, while the flying bomb began its climb to operational height at a rate of about 150m (492ft) per minute. The guidance system corrected its course as it went, and the aneroid capsule reset the elevators for level flight when the pre-determined altitude was reached.

The Fieseler Fi 103 A-1, the original and technically most common version of the flying bomb, was about 8m (26ft) long. Its wingspan was of around 5m (17ft) although there were two different wings produced in slightly different form and dimensions, and it had a maximum fuselage diameter of 0.84m (2.75ft); the warhead comprised 830kg (1832lb) of Trialen (amatol), which was sometimes supplemented by incendiary bombs. Provision was made to replace the explosive with gas, though this never happened in practice. A full load of 75–80 octane fuel added 515kg (1133lb) to the all-up launch weight total of 2180kg (4806lb). It had an autonomous range of 240km (150 miles) at a maximum speed of 645km/h (400mph), and an operational ceiling of 3000m (9800ft). It was fabricated from sheet steel pressings, with an aluminium nosecone and sheet-steel wings around a single tubular steel spar. The emphasis was on keeping costs to a minimum, and little effort was put into reducing weight by employing more exotic materials. In 1945, the Fi 103 F-1 was produced. Basically similar to the A-1, its warhead contained

Below: Very few V1s were recovered intact after they had been brought down, but some failed to explode and gave up their secrets instead. Here, RAF personnel are seen examining one in a bean field, somewhere in Kent.

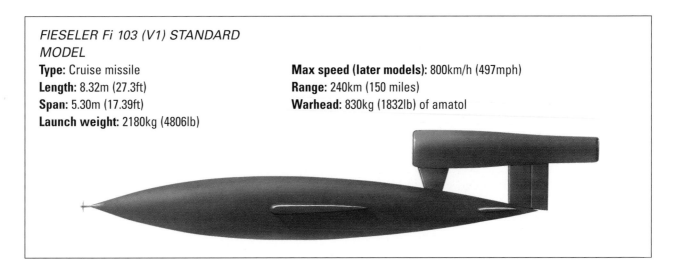

FIESELER Fi 103 (V1) STANDARD MODEL
Type: Cruise missile
Length: 8.32m (27.3ft)
Span: 5.30m (17.39ft)
Launch weight: 2180kg (4806lb)

Max speed (later models): 800km/h (497mph)
Range: 240km (150 miles)
Warhead: 830kg (1832lb) of amatol

Above: The Fieseler Fi 103, to give the V1 its official name, was unleashed in earnest against England in Operation Boxroom, which began in June 1944.

436kg (962lb) of amatol, and its fuel tanks were enlarged from 568 litres (125 gallons) to 756 litres (166 gallons), increasing range to 370km (230 miles).

THE V1 CAMPAIGN BEGINS

The first operational V1s were launched in the early hours of 13 June 1944. Just 10 missiles were deployed: four crashed immediately; two fell into the sea; and four hit the Home Counties (one in Sussex, one near Sevenoaks in Kent, one in the south-eastern suburbs of London, and one in Bethnal Green, north of the Thames). Two days later, *Unternehmen Rumpelkammer* (Operation Boxroom) commenced in earnest, and between 2200 hours on 15 June and 12 noon the following day, 244 V1s were launched, most of them against London and some against Southampton which was the re-supply base for the invasion force, even then trying to fight its way out of the beachhead in Normandy. More than half of the flying bombs launched (144 in all) crossed the English coast, and 34 were shot down by anti-aircraft guns and fighter aircraft.

This campaign from launch sites in the Pas de Calais continued until the end of August, by which time Allied troops were closing in. The Luftwaffe's Flakregiment 155 (W), its name a cover like the FZG 76 designation, had been set up in August 1943 under the command of Colonel Max Wachtel, and it packed up and moved to Holland with the intention of concentrating activities on Antwerp. By that time, it had launched 9017 missiles, 6725 of which had reached England. As many as 2340 landed in the Greater Lon-

don area, the vast majority of them exploding as planned. Other reports suggest that 8892 missiles were launched with the UK as their target during the entire war, and still others put the total at fractionally over 10,000. As early as 7 July, the ground launches had been supplemented by air launches from Heinkel He 111 bombers of III/KG 3, based at Gilze Rijen in Holland, which carried one missile each on a pylon located just outboard of the starboard wing root, and launched it at an altitude of 450m (1500ft) over the North Sea. By the end of August, over 400 missiles had been deployed in this way, mostly against London, but some against Southampton and Bristol.

Air-launched operations against targets in the United Kingdom recommenced in mid-September in a campaign which lasted until mid-January. A total of around 1200 missiles were launched (some of them at targets as far north as Manchester, though only one reached that particular objective), but only around 20 per cent of them got through to populated areas and just 66 landed on London, still the prime target in the UK. During the same period, around 1600 missiles were air-launched against Antwerp and Brussels. In all, they cost the Luftwaffe 80 aircraft shot down.

On 3 March 1945, a new campaign against London started from sites in Holland, using F-1 missiles with greater fuel capacity and a smaller warhead, but this was of only very limited success. The last flying bomb landed in London on 29 March. In all, a total of 2419 V1s had hit London and 2448 had struck Antwerp (though these were not the only targets, of course), representing roughly 25 per cent of those launched. It is estimated that V1 rockets were responsible for the deaths of perhaps 12,000 people. Official figures put the death toll in the UK at 6184, with 17,981 injured. Altogether, around 34,000 V1s were

produced, by Fieseler, Volkswagen (initially with a marked lack of success), and 'Mittelwerke', the underground factory at Nordhausen in the Harz mountains staffed almost exclusively by slave labour. The V1 was very cost-effective, even if it was at best only 20 per cent effective. Estimates of the unit cost vary, but around 5000 Reichsmarks seems reasonable at a time when the standard German infantry rifle, the Mauser 98K, was costing RM56, and a PzKpfw IV tank over RM100,000.

Above: The Reichenberg IV, seen here, was the operational version of the manned flying bomb, with a warhead but without the landing skid on its belly or flaps on the trailing surface of the wings. None was ever flown in combat.

Below: The Japanese Navy also worked on a manned flying bomb, the Yokosuka MXY7 'Ohka'. Simpler than the Reichenberg, it had rocket boosters to accelerate its gliding attack and only rudimentary flight controls.

YOKOSUKA MXY7 'OHKA'
Type: Single-seat suicide missile
Length: 6.066m (19.9ft)
Span: 5.12m (16.8ft)
Max take-off weight: 2140kg (4718lb)

Max speed: 649km/h (403mph) at 3500m (11,482ft)
Range: 37km (23 miles)
Warhead: 1200kg (2646lb) of explosives

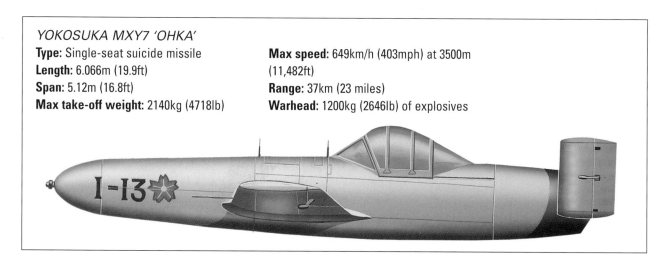

Left: A complete V1 weighed some 2.032 tonnes (2 tons), and it was customary to manhandle it into position at the foot of the ramp on its launch cradle.

THE SELBSTOPFERMÄNNER BOMBER

Desperate times breed desperate men, and both remaining arms of the Axis began to consider formalised suicide tactics, perhaps from as early as late 1943. The most famous of these was the Japanese Kamikaze (Divine Wind) campaign against ships of the Royal and US Navies from the time of the Battle of Leyte Gulf (23–26 October 1944), but Germany, too, made preparations for the use of such tactics, the most significant of those involving a manned version of the Fi 103 flying bomb. This was actually the first vehicle considered, but it was rejected in favour of a glider version of the Me 328, while a unit equipped with Fw 190s, known as 'Kommando Lange', or the 'Staffel Leonidas', was formed to begin training for missions which involved the pilot placing his aircraft – carrying the maximum possible bombload – in a steep dive aimed at the target before baling out and taking to his parachute. Eventually, the Me 328 project lost momentum, and it became clear that the chances of penetrating anti-aircraft defences in a Fw 190 carrying a sufficient bombload to be effective were extremely slim.

Attention returned to the use of the Fi 103. Designs for four different versions were worked up by DFS, and Henschel converted four standard V1 missiles. The operational codename for the project was 'Reichenberg', and the four versions of the aircraft received 'R' prefixes, I through to IV. The Fi 103 R-I was a single-seater with ballast in place of its warhead; it had skids and landing flaps, but no motor: it was constructed for the test programme. The R-II was similar, but with a second cockpit in the nose section. The R-III was designed for advanced training, and was essentially the R-I equipped with an engine. The R-IV was the operational model, with no landing aids but with ailerons, and with the warhead reinstated. There are suggestions that the warhead might have been replaced with a cannon and the aircraft used as an interceptor, too. About 175 are thought to have been built in all.

The test pilots for the development programme were Heinz Kensche and the ubiquitous Hanna Reitsch, and they reported favourably on the aircraft's performance in flight (though there were hair-raising moments, apparently) but were not so enthusiastic about landing it. One can imagine that landing was hardly a consideration as these aircraft were never meant to be landed after use, except on training flights. The intention was for the pilot to aim the aircraft at its target and then bale out, but frankly, the arrangements made for him (or her) to exit the aircraft were somewhat cynical. The cockpit was located well aft – aft of the trailing edge of the wings – and almost underneath the motor's air intake, against which it jammed before it had been opened through the 45 degrees necessary to jettison it. Even if the pilot succeeded in freeing it, he would have had little chance of levering himself out of the cockpit in a steep dive at speeds in excess of 1000km/h (620mph) without being seriously injured, if not killed. Although thousands volunteered for the *Selbstopfermänner* bomber programme and 70 were accepted for training, they were never asked to go into action, so in the final analysis, it is not important. Japanese pilots who flew the 'Ohka' flying bombs in the latter stages of the Kamikaze campaign were treated more honestly: they were sealed into their aircraft and knew they had no chance of getting out. The efficacy of the Japanese Kamikaze campaign gives some indication of the sort of results they were expected to achieve. Between 21 February and 15 August 1945, 17 ships were sunk and 198 damaged for the loss of 930 aircraft, both flying bombs and escorts.

THE 'AGGREGAT' ROCKETS

In the aftermath of the defeat of 1918, Germany was severely limited in terms of the weapons she could possess. As we noted earlier, there was a large-scale campaign to circumvent the restrictions imposed by the Treaty of Versailles by establishing development programmes abroad, but there were other avenues open, too; for instance, as early as 1929, the *Heereswaffenamt* began to look into rocketry as an alternative to long-range artillery, and set up a trials and proving ground about 32km (20 miles) south of Berlin at Kummersdorf. Captain Walter Dornberger, a professional soldier who had been sent by the Army to the School of Technology at Charlottenberg, and had earned an MA in ballistics there, was put in charge of the project in 1930 under the HWA's head, Karl Becker, himself very enthusiastic.

In 1927, a group of keen amateurs, centred on Hermann Oberth, author of *Die Rakete zu den Planetenräumen* (*The Rocket into Interplanetary Space*), published in 1923, formed the Society for Space Travel, the *Verein für Raumschiffahrt*. They began to experiment with rocket motors, and were funded initially by

Above: The launch pad at the Peenemünde research station, deep in the pine forests of the island of Usedom on the remote Baltic coast. All the test flights of the A4 were initiated from this site.

Fritz von Opel (who, we may recall, had commissioned a rocket-powered glider from Alexander Lippisch, and had also built a rocket-assisted car, the RAK 2), and funded latterly by a 10,000-franc prize Oberth won in 1929 for his book *Wege zur Raumschiffahrt* (*Ways to Spaceflight*). In 1930, a promising student named Wernher von Braun joined the Society and the following year, they successfully flew a small rocket fuelled by liquid oxygen and petrol. By then, funds were running short, but fortuitously, the Society was approached by Dornberger, who arranged for them to receive a series of small grants. In 1932, von Braun, just graduated from the Berlin Technical Institute with a BSc in mechanical engineering, went to

work at Kummersdorf and by December 1934, his group had launched two liquid-oxygen- and alcohol-fuelled rockets, designated A2, which had reached altitudes of over 2500m (8200ft).

In 1935, work started on a new rocket, the A3, which weighed 750kg (1655lb) and stood 7.6m (25ft) tall. It, too, was fuelled by A-Stoff (liquid oxygen, at −183 degrees C) and M-Stoff (methyl alcohol, or methanol), but this time the motor produced 1500kg

Right: A technician is photographed making last-minute adjustments to the guidance system prior to launching an A4 rocket, which has been brought to the vertical position by the mobile erector.

(3300lb) of thrust for 45 seconds instead of the 300kg (660lb) for 16 seconds of the A2. More important, perhaps, was the new method of stabilisation which von Braun's team devised. Whereas the A2 was stabilised by its centre section being spun by an electric motor to create a gyroscopic effect, the A3 would have small molybdenum 'rudders' (more accurately, vanes) acting to deflect a portion of the exhaust stream under the control of gyroscopes. The A3 also had four rudimentary tail fins, though these hardly extended outside the diameter of the body. Its payload consisted of an instrumentation package, and it was to return to earth on a parachute. The first A3 launch took place on 6 December 1937 from the island of Greifswalder Oie, off the Baltic coast. The new stabilisers worked, but other elements of the design, in particular the overall aerodynamics, were faulty, and the rocket was never entirely a success, although three examples were launched.

THE MOVE TO PEENEMUNDE

By then, the research group was fast outgrowing the facilities at Kummersdorf. The A2s were actually launched from the island of Borkum, off the mouth of the River Ems in the North Sea. In early 1936, the HWA and the RLM joined forces to purchase a large area of suitable land, an isolated peninsula around the village of Peenemünde on the island of Usedom, off the Baltic coast close to the present-day border with Poland. They also bought the adjacent Greifswalder Oie, and it was to this location that both moved their rocket development programmes. The Army were located to the east of the site, in an area known as *Heeresversuchsanstalt-Peenemünde* (HVP), and referred to as *Electromechanische Werke* (EMW) as a cover, where Dornberger was appointed Head of Weapon Test Section 11, with von Braun as his Technical Director. It was here that the first successful ballistic missiles the world had ever seen were developed and tested, and the name Peenemünde soon took on a new significance.

After the failure of the A3 to live up to expectations, development work on the A4, which was always intended to be a military rocket, was halted. Instead, von Braun turned to the design of another research rocket, the A5, somewhat larger than the A3 but with the same motor. The main difference between these and the earlier design was to be in the profile of its flight path, because now the requirement was not simply to send a rocket straight up into the atmosphere, but to launch it at a terrestrial target hundreds of kilometres away, and for that, a sophisticated guidance package was required. In the case of a small device like the V1, basic direction was simply a matter of aligning the launch ramp with the azimuth of the target, and then relying on a gyrocompass to apply small corrections. But steering the ballistic missile to its target would be quite another matter, since it would have to be launched vertically, and then tipped over in the precise direction of the target to an angle of 41 degrees from the horizontal and maintained there. Range was determined by the length of the burn, and that meant that propellant cut-off had to be precise and instantaneous. Cut-off was actuated initially by a radio signal from the ground, and was the only external factor applied after the launch sequence had been initiated (and this, too, being later automated). With-

Below: The RAF launched a major raid on Peenmünde on the night of 17/18 August 1943, and caused considerable damage, particularly to accommodation blocks. Both slave labourers and research staff died in the raid.

out going too far into the intricacies of the matter, to achieve a proper degree of directional stability in a ballistic missile it is necessary to be able to control its movement in three axes: pitch (to achieve and maintain the proper angle of climb); yaw (side-to-side movement, to correct the heading); and spin, which is a natural tendency of a cylindrical body in motion, but which makes controlling pitch and yaw by means of rudders almost impossible, and which must be damped out. To make matters worse, the characteristics of the missile – in particular the all-important centre of gravity – change as its fuel is consumed, and its flight characteristics change no less drastically as it climbs into and through the upper atmosphere and then descends again on its parabolic course.

EPOCH-MAKING RESEARCH

All in all, the problems of guidance were the most complex Wernher von Braun's team had to face, and they solved them definitively and, we may add, with nothing more sophisticated than slide-rules and mechanical calculators; it is perhaps significant that some of the first simple computers were produced to solve ballistic problems. The team used three-axis gyroscopes controlling small rudders built into the tips of the fins, supplemented by deflector vanes,

Above: Many of the A4s captured intact found their way to the United States (as did most of the development team). This A4 is being readied for launch, probably at the White Sands Proving Ground, New Mexico.

made now of graphite rather than molybdenum, in the exhaust stream during the first few seconds of flight, when the airflow over the conventional control surfaces was insufficient. The team's work on the remote north coast of Germany under increasingly difficult conditions between 1938 and 1945 was actually to change civilisation itself – if not in the sense that at least some of them intended – by enabling man to leave earth for the first time.

During 1938, work proceeded on the new design, and by the year's end, four unguided launches had been made to a distance of 17km (10.6 miles), and an altitude of 11,000m (36,000ft). Work on the guidance system continued. By October 1939, a month or so into World War II, the guidance and control package – in fact, every essential component of the A4 except its warhead and motor – had been assembled in the rocket, and test firing commenced. The results were successful, and in early 1940 Dornberger thankfully ordered work on the A4 to begin once again, with a production target date of mid-1943. He bargained without Adolf Hitler.

By July 1940, it seemed that Hitler's war would be over by the year's end, with virtually all of Europe under his control, the Soviet Union pacified by treaty, and Britain isolated. It was then that the Führer gave the fateful order to cancel any research project which could not be guaranteed to show results within 12 months. One of the first casualties was Dornberger's war rocket. Or so, at any rate, went the theory. In fact, Dornberger managed to evade the directive by continuing to work on individual components, including the 25,000kg- (55,125lb-) thrust engine, and was also able to continue the A5 programme, which was still supplying much-needed data on flight characteristics.

In fact, test firings of the new motor, the brainchild of Dr Walter Thiel, had already begun. These tests had revealed that there would be additional problems in its operation, relating purely to scale, particularly in

cooling it and supplying it with sufficient fuel. The calculations had shown that to obtain the required thrust, it would be necessary to deliver almost 125kg (275lb) of fuel to the combustion chamber every second. The earlier rockets had required very much less, and it had been sufficient to pressurise the propellant tanks with nitrogen. But now it was necessary to devise a means of actually pumping the fuel and the liquid oxygen from tank to burner. The method chosen was a steam turbine, and the means of generating the steam was the same as that used in the V1's launch catapult: the near-explosive decomposition of T-Stoff into super-heated steam when it came into contact with the catalyst Z-Stoff. The turbine thus powered produced around 675hp and ran at 5000rpm.

TO THE MARGINS OF SPACE

Thanks to a long catalogue of setbacks (and, we may imagine, the need to keep the project at least partially hidden from those who would have preferred more resources to have gone into their own laboratories), the hand-built prototype A4 was not ready for static testing until 18 March 1942, and even then, it exploded. Von Braun's team built another one, which exploded too, but eventually they managed to make enough progress to dare a test flight. Scheduled for 13 June, it was a failure. Von Braun returned if not to the drawing board, at least to the workshop, and readied another prototype. After a second failed test launch, on 16 August, happily for von Braun and Dornberger, the third attempt on 3 October proved more successful. The missile flew over 200km (125 miles) to an altitude of 85km (53 miles) and thus into the ionosphere at the margins of space; it returned to earth within 4km (2.5 miles) of its intended target. Now all that remained was to sell the concept as a weapon of war; by late 1942 that was not much of a problem.

Hitler endorsed the V2 programme, as it soon became known, on 22 December. It was held up by shortages of strategic materials and by the RAF, which sent a mixed force of 596 aircraft to drop 1828 tonnes (1800 tons) of bombs on Peenemünde on the night of 17 August, losing 40 aircraft and killing around 800 people on the ground – most of them conscripted Polish labourers, but including Dr Thiel – and setting back the programme by perhaps two

months. It had seemed for a while that the Army-sponsored A4 would lose out to the Air Force's Fi 103, but a demonstration of both before high-ranking government officials in May 1943 came at a bad time for the latter, and the A4 programme survived. As the war situation worsened that year, Hitler became more and more interested in the A4, eventually giving it the highest priority, allocating production facilities at one of Henschel's factories and at the Zeppelin works at Friedrichshafen. Both sites were bombed before production could start up, in fact, and A4s were instead assembled at the 'Mittelwerke' underground factory at Nordhausen from components manufactured all over occupied Europe. First deliveries were made in July 1944, and from September, the month when the V2 campaign started, a steady output of over 600 a month was maintained. Meanwhile, a training and test unit was established and launch sites were selected.

There were two opposing views as to how the V2s should be deployed. The *Oberkommando des Heeres* (OKH – Army High Command) wanted huge, well-protected fixed sites, and selected three locations in Northern France from which rockets could be launched against England. The first of these, at Watten, near St Omer, was destroyed by the USAAF on 27 August 1943 while construction was still in an early phase; the second, at Siracourt, and the third, in a quarry at Wizernes, were truly massive affairs, over one million tonnes (one million tons) of reinforced concrete being cast into a protective dome, beneath which storage and launch chambers, and accommodation, were hollowed out. They were both destroyed by the RAF in July 1944 as part of Operation Crossbow (the broader campaign to destroy the V1 launch sites) using 'Tallboy' penetration bombs, and finished off with remotely controlled B-17 Flying Fortresses, packed with explosive, the following month. With that, the thoughts of the high command turned to the sort of mobile launchers that Dornberger had been advocating all along.

30-VEHICLE BATTERY

Given the complexity of the missile itself, the launch procedure was quite straightforward. One of the trucks in the battery's 30-vehicle convoy carried a circular launch platform fabricated from steel, which incorporated a blast deflector. This was set up on the ground at the rear of the missile transporter and levelled by means of screw jacks in its four legs. The FR-Anhänger-S missile transporter, commonly known as the 'Meillerwagen' after its manufacturer, was

Left: Some captured A4 rockets were launched from sites in Germany into the German test target zones. Here, British personnel prepare to launch a V2 using the original equipment, including the 'Meillerwagen' erector/launcher.

secured to it. While the power and test cables were being run out from the generator and control trucks, two of the three straps retaining the missile on its trailer bed were removed, leaving the topmost in place, and the nose fuze was then inserted. An auxiliary motor provided power for the hydraulic rams which then raised the missile to the vertical position – a process which took about 12 minutes – and when it was hanging vertically over the launch platform, the latter was jacked up to take the missile's weight and the top retaining strap was removed.

The various cables were then connected up, the transporter withdrew a short distance so that hinged platforms on its gantry could be deployed as work stations, and the testing procedure began. Once this had been successfully completed, the fuelling crews went to work, filling the main tanks with liquid oxygen and methanol and the smaller tanks with hydrogen peroxide and the permanganate catalyst. Then the launch

platform was rotated on its base to align the missile with the target (the process of tipping it in flight was carried out by spinning a drum around its horizontal axis, thus causing the missile to rotate slowly in the opposite direction; the axis of the drum had, therefore, to be precisely at right-angles to the azimuth of the target). Lastly, the igniter – a small firework, set off electrically – was wedged into the tail pipe, and the set-up crews withdrew.

Right: In addition to the 'Meillerwagen' and its fleet of associated vehicles, A4 launch teams also employed special trains. They were somewhat less flexible logistically but smoother in operation.

Below: The A4 rocket – even without its 975kg (2150lb) warhead filled with amatol mix – could make a very large hole in the ground indeed... This crater was the result of a test firing at White Sands.

The armoured launch control booth was situated in the back of a half-track vehicle, based on either the SdKfz 11 Leichter Zugkraftwagen or the similar SdKfz 251 Mittlerer Schützenpanzerwagen, the armoured maid-of-all-work of the German Army since 1944. Closing the firing switch opened the valves in the T-Stoff and Z-Stoff tanks and set the turbine pump in motion. Once it was up to speed, the main valves were opened, feeding propellant to the combustion chamber, and the igniter was fired. Directional control in the first few seconds was achieved by the carbon vanes in the exhaust gas flow, but as the rocket's speed increased, the external fin-tip rudders took over. As the missile rose, the spin of the drum caused it to tip over slowly, and at the appropriate point, the propellant supply was cut, initially by radio signal, later by command from an accelerometer. The warhead was armed only during flight, about 60 seconds after lift-off at the moment of propellant cut-off,

Below: As this cutaway diagram shows, most of the internal volume of the A4 was taken up with tanks containing the liquid oxygen and methanol it used as fuel.

and there was an interlock in the arming system which prevented arming taking place if the right conditions were not met. There was no provision for destroying the missile in flight on command.

TARGET PARIS

There were five batteries in all, based around the Hague in Holland – one from Artillerie Abteilung (AA) 444, two from AA 485 and two from AA 836. The first and last formed the Southern Group, and operated against targets in France and Belgium, while AA 485 formed the Northern Group and was tasked with targeting England. It was AA 444 which launched the first operational V2, against Paris on 5 September 1944. Three days later, AA 485 fired two rockets aimed at London, the first of which hit Staveley Road, Chiswick, in west London – having been aimed at Southwark, 13km (8 miles) away – at just before 1845 hours in the evening, demolishing six houses, killing three people and injuring 17. The campaign against London was to last exactly 200 days, the last missile falling at 1920 hours on 27 March 1945, hitting a block of flats in Whitechapel, killing

PEENEMUNDE A4 (V2)
Type: Long-range ballistic missile
Length: 14.05m (46.09ft)
Diameter: 1.68m (5.51ft)
Lift-off weight: 12,870kg (28,373lb)
Speed: 5580km/h (3465mph)
Max range: 330km (205 miles)
Warhead: 975kg (2150lb) of amatol mix

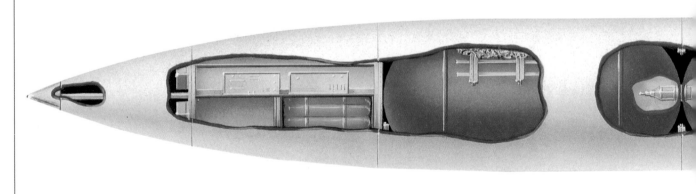

134. Other reports suggest that the last A4 launched against London actually fell in Orpington, Kent, that day. In those 200 days, out of 1120 launched, 1054 rockets landed in England, 517 of them in the Greater London area, and, according to official figures, killed 2754 people and injured 6532. The larger Southern Group fired rather more missiles in all (about 1675), most of them targeted against Antwerp (1341). It also directed its fire against Brussels, Liège, Luxembourg, Paris and the Rhine crossing at Remagen. There was, of course, no defence against the V2. Only the Allied advance across northern Europe, which drove the Mobile Artillery Battalions out of range of worthwhile targets, put a stop to the campaign. Gruppe Nord reportedly still had 60 unexpended missiles when it fell back into Germany on 29 March.

It is worth noting that a project aimed at firing an A4 from a submerged U-boat (actually, from a self-contained chamber it towed behind it, which was caused to float vertically by means of flooding its tail section) had reached a fairly advanced stage by 1945, with several containers having been completed and tested at the Vulkan shipyard in Stettin. Known as Project Test-Stand XII, and conceived apparently by Volkswagen in late 1944, this was aimed at the bombardment of New York. However, it is suggested that a more-or-less successful test firing in the Baltic made it clear that a fully fuelled missile (there was no way it could be fuelled at sea) could not be expected to stand up to the rigours of a trans-Atlantic voyage, even submerged. The project was shelved.

The A4 missile in its final form was to be made entirely of steel. At just over 14m (46ft) long, with a maximum body diameter of 1.68m (5.5ft) and a span over its fins of 3.5m (11.5ft), it weighed 12,870kg (28,373lb), of which 975kg (2150lb) of amatol comprised its warhead, and 4900kg (10,780lb) of liquid oxygen and 3770kg (8300lb) of methanol comprised the bulk of its propellant. It had a maximum range of 330km (205 miles), which it covered in 3 minutes 40 seconds (of which it was under power for 70 seconds), reaching a maximum velocity of 5580km/h (3465mph) and height of 96,000m (315,000ft). Its velocity at impact was 2900km/h (1800 mph). There are rather divergent figures for total A4 production, estimates ranging from 6000 to as many as 10,000.

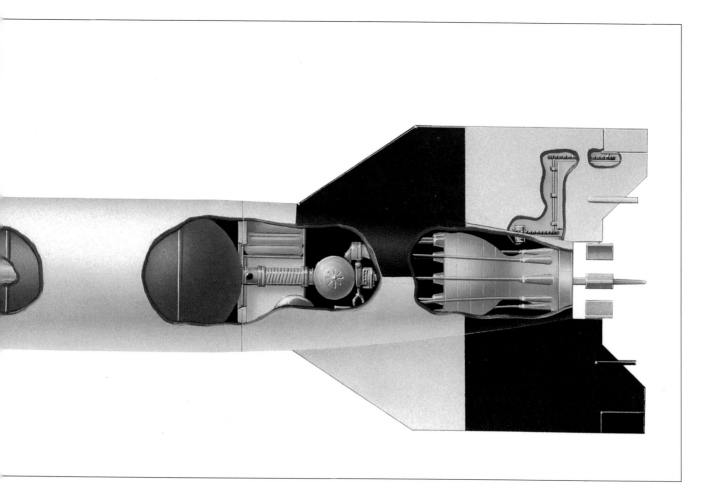

Above: An A4 rocket, shrouded in tarpaulin, on the railway flatcar used to transport it to the vicinity of the launch site. The Allied advance across northern Europe drove the V2 battalions out of effective range of worthwhile targets.

THE LATER GUIDED BALLISTIC MISSILE PROJECTS

As soon as the A4 was viable, the project was taken out of von Braun's hands. He and his team, it is suggested, were never entirely satisfied with it, and would happily have gone on refining their design, but Heinrich Himmler, who had previously seized control of all the secret weapons programmes, would not accept that. Von Braun turned to working on ways of increasing its range. The simplest means, he concluded, was to fit it with wings, so that it would glide in the final phase of its flight, prolonging its descent and increasing its range to 435km (270 miles), but he counted without the effects of re-entering the dense air at lower atmospheric levels. The one A4b missile which was launched successfully (the first one crashed soon after take-off) failed to re-enter cleanly and was destroyed.

The A6, which never made it past the discussion stage, was to have been an A4 fueled by SV-Stoff, made up of 94 per cent nitric acid and 6 per cent nitrous oxide, and Visol (the generic name given to a group of isobutyl-vinyl esters); it was to have 20 per

cent more thrust. The A7 was a winged version of the A5, air-launched as a concept vehicle for the A9. The A8 was virtually identical to the A6 but fuelled with SV-Stoff and diesel oil, although it is also suggested that it was to have been fuelled with LOX and methanol contained in pressurized tanks, rather than employing the turbine pump to deliver them to the combustion chamber. The A9 was the A4b with modified wing planform: essentially, the horizontal fins were to have been continued forward, right to the rocket's nose, in a simple ogive, to allow it to survive re-entry; it had the motor from the A6, with a projected range of 600km (370 miles).

The final ballistic missile project, the A10, was much more ambitious in scale and had it ever materialised, would have been the first ever ICBM. The projected inter-continental ballistic missile was to have been a two-stage rocket, the first stage being based on six A4 motors linked into a common venturi, and designed to propel its second stage – either an A4 or an A9 – to an altitude of 24km (14.9 miles) before its own motor was fired, giving it a range of around 4800km (2800 miles) with a 1000kg (2200lb) amatol warhead and a flight time of around 45 minutes. It is suggested that this project was first discussed as early as 1940, long before the United States entered the war, but there is no evidence that it got beyond the discussion stage. There was also talk of modifying the second-stage A9 missile to carry a pilot, who would have been ejected once he had locked the missile on a course for its target (presumably he would have been recovered by a submarine), but that idea can be dismissed as a flight of fancy.

THE 'RHEINBOTE' ROCKET

The FZG 76 and the A4 were the only guided surface-to-surface missiles employed by either side during World War II, but the A4 was by no means the only war rocket. Most of the combatant nations employed much simpler devices – unguided and with solid-fuel 'motors' – as adjuncts to their artillery or as assault weapons, but once again, only Germany went one stage further, and produced a long-range unguided ballistic missile, the Rh.Z.61/9 'Rheinbote' ('Rhine Messenger'), developed by a company better known for its artillery pieces and its share in the development of the superlative MG 42 general-purpose machine gun, Rheinmetall-Borsig. Where the A4 was complex and expensive, 'Rheinbote' was simple. It was a fin-stabilised four-stage solid-fuel rocket, each of the first

three stages igniting the next as it burned out and fell away, with no guidance system, but relying on simple alignment of the launch rail with the target. The launch rail could be mounted on either a high-angle 8.8cm anti-aircraft gun mount or on a modified 'Meillerwagen', and the complete missile was almost 11.5m (37.5ft) long with a maximum body diameter (in the first stage) of 535mm (21.1in) and a maximum fin span of 1.49m (58.5in). It weighed a total of 1715kg (3775lb), almost a third of which was propellant. It had a maximum range of 220km (140 miles) when fired at an elevation of 65 degrees, the final stage, with its 40kg (88lb) warhead, attaining a speed of Mach 5.5 (almost 6000km/h; 3730mph) and climbing to a maximum altitude of 78km (48.5 miles). Over 200 of these missiles were fired at Antwerp in November 1944.

Below: An A4 rocket is paraded through London's Trafalgar Square in late September 1945. The rocket was reportedly captured in France, and was later set up as if for launch next to Nelson's Column. Greater London was on the receiving end of more than 500 V2s in 1944–45.

CHAPTER SIX

Air-to-Air Weapons

While the adoption of the machine gun made air-to-air combat feasible, by the mid-years of World War II, it had come close to causing a stand-off: machine gun- (and even cannon-) armed aircraft dared not approach each other: it was too dangerous. The alternative, it was clear to German researchers, was to develop small rocket-propelled flying bombs which could be directed to their targets via either wire-borne or radio signals from a chase plane which stayed outside the lethal area.

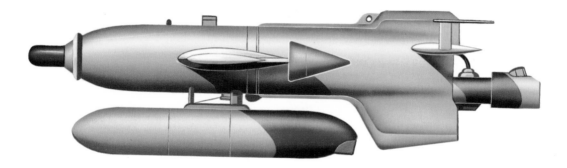

During his post-war interrogation, Generalleutnant Adolf Galland described the many and various weapons the Luftwaffe had used – or had contemplated using – against the tightly packed formations of Allied daylight bombers with their heavy defensive firepower. He described how attacking the formations from the rear immediately resulted in heavy casualties, and how the German interceptors then switched over to attacking them head-on, hoping to break up the formation and then go after consequently vulnerable individual aircraft. This worked up to a point, but only until the bombers began taking concerted evasive action, and from then – some time in the winter of 1942–43 – the Luftwaffe began looking at alternatives

Above: Henschel developed the Hs 293 for use against shipping, but an air-to-air variant was also produced.

Left: Germany desperately needed an antidote to massed formations of Allied bombers like these B-17s.

to the simple cannon and machine gun to arm their aircraft, to allow them to attack either from unexpected directions or from outside the effective range of the Fortress's and Liberator's .5 inch Brownings. Because the bombers flew so close together, much consideration was given to bombing them, and a variety of methods were tested, including dive-bombing individual aircraft; towing command-detonated 10kg (22lb) fragmentation bombs on long cables (tested in combat, with two unconfirmed successes, despite the physical difficulty of actually delivering the weapon, which trailed out behind the towing aircraft); and dropping blast and fragmentation bombs on parachutes ahead of the formation to form an aerial minefield (this latter method was promising, but development of a satisfactory weapon came too late). Other methods included using forward-firing heavy cannon – essentially, light anti-aircraft and anti-tank guns – to shoot at them from a great distance, but this was to prove only marginally effective; and using

Above: The simplest of all air-to-air missiles was the unguided rocket, fired in a salvo. This Ba 349 was armed with 24 R4M rockets with 250g (8.8oz) warheads.

obliquely firing cannon to attack them from below. This approach was to prove devastatingly effective against RAF night bombers, but less so against the USAAF, whose aircraft had belly and waist gunners.

One of the reasons that heavy forward-firing guns were ineffective was the amount of recoil they produced: it slowed the aircraft perceptibly if more than a few rounds were fired. The effect should not be underestimated. One trainee in an Me 262, who found himself committed to landing on too short a strip, let go with the four 30mm MK 108 in the aircraft's nose and brought his aircraft up short of the end of the runway, thanks to the additional braking effect. Another reason was the extra drag these usually externally mounted guns created, reducing the aircraft's performance considerably. For the Germans, the employment of relatively heavy calibre guns in aircraft seems to have had a lasting fascination. Other nations' air forces tried it too; the ultimate in that line, according to one source, seems to have been the fitting of a 32pdr (94mm) anti-tank gun into a Mosquito. For the Germans, the programme to adapt light anti-aircraft guns and anti-tank guns – notably in 3.7cm and 5cm calibres, though 7.5cm was tested, too – continued to the war's end. Some of the last German aircraft left in combat were a pair of Me 262A-1a/U4s with the 5cm

Mauser MK 214 mounted in the nose. One of these aircraft, nicknamed 'Wilma Jeanne' was captured intact by US forces, but was destroyed after it suffered engine failure during a flight to Cherbourg, where it was to have been loaded aboard a ship for the USA.

There was an alternative: the so-called 'recoilless rifle', invented during World War I by an American naval officer named Davis. A variety of recoilless rifles were mounted on aircraft and tested, but though the type worked well enough in principle – and one, it is reported, was used successfully in combat – this was a single-shot weapon, with all the problems thereof. In fact we may bear in mind that the only reason air-to-air combat had ever been even possible was thanks to the machine gun, with its unique ability to keep on throwing bullets into a target area until something ran into one or more of them. The weapons in question were of two basic types. The simpler type worked on the counter-shot principle and was almost two guns in one. The 'ordinary' barrel contained the projectile; a subsidiary barrel behind the breech, precisely aligned with the regular barrel, contained a counter-shot of the same weight, usually composed of wax or grease and lead shot in a paper cartridge. In between them lay the chamber containing the propellant cartridge. When the gun was fired, both projectile and counter-shot left their respective barrels with the same energy, and their recoils thus cancelled each other out. In the more refined (and more complex) version of the weapon, the cartridge case became the counter-shot, its lesser mass being compensated for by allowing a proportion of the propellant gases to be exhausted through a series of jets in the chamber wall, the components once again cancelling each other out. Both methods worked, though the latter caused some bad moments for pilots who flew aircraft so equipped.

THE ZOSSEN DEVICE

The Luftwaffe tried to surmount the problem of the weapon being able to fire only a single round by mounting it in groups of as many as 49, to be set off in ripple salvoes. Recoilless guns were mounted to fire both forwards and upwards; pilots of single-seater aircraft found aiming the latter to be somewhat problematic, and so a trigger unit which incorporated a light source and a photoelectric cell, the so-called 'Zossen' device, was developed. It was tested successfully in 1944, but very few were ever fitted to aircraft. An even more complicated automatic trigger was developed for a downward-firing recoilless rifle for use against tanks, detecting the tank's magnetic field and using that to trigger the gun when the aircraft was directly overhead.

Perhaps the most ambitious plan ever involving gun armament for aircraft was put forward early in 1939. The Gerät 104 was a 35cm-calibre recoilless gun which fired a 635kg (1400lb) armour-piercing shell (the cartridge case weighed the same, and thus acted as the counter-shot itself). It was intended for use against ships of the Royal Navy lying at anchor in Scapa Flow (a place of special importance to the Germans, of course, not just because it dominated the northern approaches, but also as the site of the scuttling of the High Seas Fleet in 1919), but in the event, the plan came to nothing. However, later an even bigger weapon, the 54cm 'Münchausen' cannon, was proposed, and it seems that a prototype was constructed and mounted beneath a Junkers Ju 87 Stuka dive-bomber. Not entirely unsurprisingly, the effect of firing such a weapon, recoilless or not, upon a relatively light aircraft was unpredictable to say the least and the project was cancelled.

Another, and simpler, solution to the recoil problem was to substitute rockets – which have no recoil – for guns, and almost from the outset, this proved to be successful. Initially, the weapon used was a cutdown version of the Army's 21cm Nebelwerfer 42 rocket launcher, mounted in various ways, which was eventually superseded by the 5.5cm R4M rocket. The 21cm rockets were first fitted in pairs to Fw 190s; they could be jettisoned after use, and most pilots

adopted this procedure, for they robbed the aircraft of about 50km/h (30mph). They were used against bomber formations, and also as air-to-ground weapons. Twin-engine fighters such as the Bf 110 and Me 410 were fitted with larger batteries. They were not only employed as forward-firing weapons; a few Ju 88s and He 177s were modified to carry up to 24 launchers within the fuselage, angled to fire upwards, while some Fw 190s carried a single rearwards-firing tube. The rocket itself, the 21cm Wurfgranate (Spreng), was a powerful weapon, with a 10.2kg (22.4lb) warhead and an intial velocity of 320m/s (1050fps). As an artillery bombardment rocket it had a range of about 8000m (8750 yards); in the air it was reckoned to be effective out to 800–1200m (875–1300 yards).

THE R4M

The R4M was more effective: with its much smaller profile it produced less drag, and more could be carried. The usual load for an Me 262 was 24, in a rack under each wing outboard of the engines, but that could be doubled when necessary by adding another pair of racks. The racks were mounted at an upwards inclination of 8 degrees, and the missiles were fired serially, at a fraction of a second's interval (a 'ripple salvo'), at a range of around 600m (660yds). The R4M was simplicity itself: a stick of diglycol solid fuel which, being nitrocellulose based, burned at a predictable rate based on the surface area exposed to the atmosphere, with a contact-fuzed warhead and spring-loaded stabilising fins, which deployed as soon as it left the launch tube (originally of metal, but later of carboard). Measuring 82cm (32.2in) long and 5.5cm (2.16in) in diameter, it was adapted for a variety of purposes but was mainly employed against aircraft and tanks. It was virtually identical to the British 3in (7.62cm) rocket which preceded it into service by some years. 'Föhn', its putative successor, was a somewhat larger but essentially similar device, originally designed as an anti-aircraft weapon. With a diameter of 7.3cm (2.8in), it had a conventional warhead containing 250g (8.8oz) of TNT/RDX (the R4M's anti-aircraft warhead, the PB-3, was a shaped-charge, with 400g (14oz) of Hexogen). Few, if any, were used operationally.

One of the advantages of the R4M was that since the rocket had the same short-range ballistics as the 30mm cannon shell, the existing cockpit gunsight could be employed, but unfortunately, that was saying very little, for it was not an easy task to take accurate aim on a target which was taking evasive action from a fast-flying aircraft whose flight characteristics caused it to snake at high speed. The answer, of course, was to provide a guidance system to control the missile in flight.

AIR-TO-AIR MISSILES

From as early as 1939, the Henschel company – a newcomer to aviation, but with a very solid background in heavy engineering – had maintained a team whose task was to study the remote control of unmanned aircraft. In January 1940, Herbert Wagner arrived to head the team, with a brief from the RLM to concentrate on air-to-surface missiles (ASMs). He was successful, as we shall discover, and in 1943 the company proposed a version of the Hs 293 ASM he developed as an air-to-air missile (AAM). Like most of the ASMs, the Hs 293H was a blast weapon, to be guided into a bomber formation and exploded there, instead of being aimed at an individual aircraft, and had a 295kg (650lb) warhead. One version of it was to have had a television camera in its nose, the picture it transmitted to the controller allowing him a clear view at ranges of up to about 4km (2.5 miles), but the apparatus proved very unreliable, and the idea, also tried out on the ASM itself, was shelved. Control was line-of-sight from the launch aircraft, the operator using a joystick to initiate radio signals which in turn actuated control surfaces on the missile itself.

This system was to be used in all the German guided missiles, and will be explained more fully below, in the context of the surface-to-air missiles for which it was originally developed. The missile had both command and proximity fuzes as well as a barometric fuze to ensure that it would self-destruct before it hit the ground. It was powered by a specially designed Schmidding rocket which used M-Stoff (methanol) and A-Stoff (oxygen), the latter being, unusually, in gaseous form, to produce 610kg (1340lb) of static thrust for 11 seconds. The Hs 293 was too big and clumsy for the anti-aircraft role, and it comes as no surprise to discover that after some initial enthusiasm, the RLM went cold on the idea. By then, however, Henschel had begun work on the 'Schmetterling' surface-to-air missile (SAM; see Chapter Eight), and had proposed a version for use in the AAM role.

THE HENSCHEL Hs 117H

The Hs 117H, as the variant was known, was very little different from the basic 'Schmetterling', save that it required no external booster rockets, but it had a significantly larger warhead, containing 100kg (220lb) of explosive. It employed the same guidance system as the Hs 293H. The intended range of the Hs 117H was 6–10km (3.7–6.2 miles), at up to 5000m (16,500ft) above the 'parent' aircraft, which was a considerable improvement over the earlier missile. It was still in development at the war's end, having survived the axe which descended on so many development projects in January 1945, it is suggested, simply because it had so much in common with the ASM from which it was descended.

Henschel also developed a missile specifically intended for use in the air-to-air role, the Hs 298, considerably smaller than either of the others and with reduced range. Like them, it had swept-back wings and a tailplane with short fins at its extremities, and control was by means of solenoid-operated 'Wagner bars' responding to radio signals. The motor was a solid-fuel two-stage Schmidding 109-543 which gave 150kg (330lb) of thrust for five-and-a-half seconds followed by 50kg (110lb) of thrust for 20 seconds. The first experimental Hs 298 was fired in May 1944, and altogether some 300 were produced and expended in trials. With a warhead containing either 25kg (55lb) or 48kg (106lb) of explosive, detonated on command or by a proximity fuze, it had a range of up to 2500m (2735 yards), travelled at either 940km/h (585mph) or 680km/h (425mph), and was designed to be deployed aboard piston-engined aircraft such as Do 217s, Fw 190s and Ju 88s. Development ceased in favour of the Ruhrstahl X-4 in January 1945.

THE RUHRSTAHL X-4

Ruhrstahl AG was, as its name suggests, a steelmaker. In 1940 it was ordered to collaborate with Dr Max Kramer of the DVL to develop a series of bombs and missiles using the spoiler control method the latter had demonstrated two years earlier. This collaboration was to result in three very interesting missiles: the so-called 'Fritz-X' guided glider bomb; the X-7 'Rottkäppchen' ('Red Riding Hood') anti-tank missile; and the X-4 air-to-air missile. Development of the X-4 began in 1943 in parallel with Henschel's Hs 298. These two missiles had very similar specifications, though it appears that the X-4 was designed from the start to operate with jet aircraft, and thus flew at higher speeds. The primary difference between the X-4 and other missiles was that it was equipped not with wings and a tailplane, but with two sets of four fins, one set swept back at an acute angle, with parallel chord width roughly halfway back from

Above: The Ruhrstahl X-4 was the most sophisticated of all the air-to-air missiles produced during World War II. It had an ingenious wire-based guidance system.

the nose; the other, offset by 45 degrees and carrying the moveable spoilers, at the tail. Secondarily, it was designed from the outset to be guided by wire, rather than radio signals – as it was planned to switch over to control by wire for all missiles since radio signals were simply too easy to jam – the necessary differentiation being obtained by switching the polarity of the signal to activate the pitch controls, and by varying its strength to activate the yaw controls. This system used the Düsseldorf/Detmold (FuG 510/238) transmitter-receiver pair, which were analogous to the Kehl/Strassburg radio transmitter and receiver. It was originally developed for use with the glide bomb, as we shall see in due course.

As we noted when discussing the surface-to-surface missiles, a cylindrical body in flight has a tendency to roll. The small fin-tip vanes necessary to correct the tendency in the X-4 would have interfered with Kramer's control spoilers, so instead of trying to correct it, the X-4's designers encouraged and controlled it to a rate of about one revolution per second by fitting offset trim tabs to the main fins. This, it was believed, had the subsidiary effect of nullifying manufacturing inaccuracies causing imbalance (which would have thrown the missile off its line) just as the rifling in a gun's barrel does. Because of the spin, though, it was necessary to fit a gyroscopic unit which switched the control signals between the spoilers on the rear fins so that those which controlled pitch while they were within 45 degrees of the horizontal changed

over to controlling yaw as they came within 45 degrees of the vertical, and vice-versa. The 5.5km- (3.5 mile-) long wires carrying the positive and return components of the electrical signal were paid out from bobbins in streamlined pods on the tips of two of the main fins. It mattered not at all that the control wires became twisted as the missile spun, for it made a maximum of perhaps 24 revolutions in the entire course of its flight. It was planned to use the liquid-fuelled BMW 109-548 rocket to power the missile, and in order to counteract any tendency the spin (and any violent manoeuvres in flight) had to disrupt fuel flow, the tanks which contained the R-Stoff and SV-Stoff were spirally wound concentrically within the double-tapering cylindrical form of the missile's body. They contained free-moving pistons – leather in the R-Stoff tank, aluminium in the acidic oxidizer – driven by compressed air. The motor, producing 140kg (310lb) of thrust reducing to 30kg (66lb) by the end of its 17-second burn time, was only ever used in some of the test launches, Schmidding 109-603 diglycol solid-fuel motors being substituted.

The first test firing of the missile from an aircraft (an Fw 190) took place on 11 August 1944, and by that time a total of 224 prototypes had been produced. In all, about 1000 airframes were then produced for operational use between August and December 1944, but there were delays in engine production. Then, just as the problems were ironed out, the BMW plant which was manufacturing the 109-548 was badly damaged in an air raid, and the motors which had been belatedly produced were destroyed. This was the final nail in the X-4's coffin and the missile never saw operational service as a result.

Air-to-Surface Missiles

Hitting a target on the ground with a bomb dropped from an aircraft was never easy; as soon as effective anti-aircraft artillery and fighter aircraft were added to the equation, it became very costly, too, particularly in human lives. By the end of the twentieth century, stand-off bombing using remote guidance was to become commonplace, but at the time of World War II this was pure fantasy – until German scientists took up the task.

During the Spanish Civil War of 1936–1939, the Luftwaffe discovered that the only really effective way to deliver bombs on to a point target was in a near-vertical dive. This procedure they repeated in 1939 in Poland and in 1940 in the Low Countries and France. Over Britain, later in the year, the Luftwaffe came across the basic flaw in this principle: dive bombers were uncomfortably vulnerable to effective

Above: The Henschel Hs 294 guided aerial torpedo's tail and wings were designed to break off on hitting the water.

Left: An early air-to-surface missile was the Blohm & Voss Bv 143, mounted here on a Heinkel He 111H.

fighter aircraft and concentrated anti-aircraft artillery. As an alternative, there was always area bombing from high altitude, but it was very wasteful and of little use against isolated high-value targets. Warships at sea were particularly difficult to hit, and the Luftwaffe frequently found itself mounting costly raids on important maritime targets which achieved little or nothing. Quite early on, thoughts turned to the development of a bomb which could be guided in flight.

THE RUHRSTAHL X-1

Ruhrstahl's X-4 air-to-air missile showed promise, but it never lived up to it. Much more useful was the guided bomb they produced as the X-1. It had a plethora of names: the RLM called it the PC 1400X; the Luftwaffe called it the 'Fritz-X'; and it has also been referred to as the FX 1400 and simply as the FX. However, its success was shortlived, despite having been designed with cheapness and simplicity in mind.

It had as its starting point the Luftwaffe's standard 1400kg (3080lb) bomb, either the cast-steel thick-cased SD (Sprengbombe Dickwändig) 1400 known as 'Fritz', or the forged-steel armour-piercing variant, the PC (Panzersprengbombe Cylindrisch) 1400. The original bomb, manufactured by Rheinmetall-Borsig, of perfectly conventional shape, was a plain cylinder with a rounded nose coming to a blunt point and a conical tail with four sheet-metal fins partially shrouded by a strengthening ring at the extremity. Ruhrstahl modified the overall form somewhat for its guided bomb, leaving the last part of the cylinder intact but introducing an oversize ogival form to the first two-thirds of its length.

In order to maximise its aerodynamic performance, they gave it four relatively large fins, located forward of the mid-point of the bomb's length, with square leading edges and a pronounced sweep to the trailing edges. These main fins were mounted asymmetrically, as if they formed the diagonals of a rectangle with sides in the ratio one-and-a-half to one. The 12-sided framework which replaced the simple fin-and-shroud empennage maintained that same basic rectangular form, but with the corners cut off. Within it were four smaller fins, set vertically and horizontally and containing the spoilers themselves, simple tabs which were actuated by electro-magnets and which caused disturbance within the airflow over the appropriate surface of the fin when they were deployed. Deployment in turn caused the whole bomb to alter course or angle of descent by swinging it around the axis formed by the straight leading edge of the main fins.

RADIO GUIDED

Guidance was by means of a radio link using the Kehl/Strassburg system (but later, the wire-link control system was adapted for use with the X-1 too), while flares, or battery-powered lamps on the tail for use at night, helped the operator to keep track of the missile in flight. It was a simple, fairly ingenious system, and it worked well enough, so long as the bomb was dropped from sufficient height. Released at the minimum altitude of 4000m (13,125ft) it had a range of up to 4.5km (2.8 miles); dropped from the maximum height any of its carrying aircraft could attain of

8000m (26,250ft), the range was up to 9km (5.6 miles). It was capable of piercing 130mm (5.125in) of armour plate when dropped from 6000m (19,700ft). Though it is often referred to as a glider bomb, that is not actually the case. Its forward speed was that imparted by the launching aircraft, and it certainly did not 'fly' in any accepted sense. Its only major vector was downwards, and all the spoilers could do was modify its path to a small degree. That was often enough to make the difference between success and failure, as we shall see later when we look at operational deployment of the ASMs. A total of 1386 X-1s were produced between April 1943 and December 1944, when manufacturing ceased, and this was far short of the planned figure of 750 per month. Less than half of them – a total of 602 – were expended, in testing, training and operations.

THE RUHRSTAHL X-1 IN ACTION

From 29 August 1943, III Gruppe/Kampfgeschwader 100 (III/KG 100), equipped with Dornier 217K-2s and operating out of Istres near Marseilles, was the first unit to employ Ruhrstahl X-1s to attack Allied shipping in the Mediterranean. Initially they were unsuccessful, but within a fortnight they had scored heavily and it soon became clear that the X-1 was a very potent weapon indeed.

On 4 September, Italy abandoned the Axis and reached a separate peace with the Allies, but there were still no clear indications of which way the powerful but until now seriously misused Italian Navy would jump. On 9 September the Allies landed at Salerno, and at 12 noon that day, reconnaissance reported that the Italian Fleet was at sea, headed south for Malta. Within two hours, 12 Do 217s of III Gruppe, led by Major Bernhard Jope, each armed with a single X-1, were in the air. They headed east at low altitude, then, climbing as they neared the coast of Sardinia, made out the shapes of three battleships with an escort of six cruisers and eight destroyers. Jope led his formation to 6500m (7108 yards) and turned towards the ships, which were now zig-zagging wildly and firing every one of their anti-aircraft guns. The first missile, launched by Oberleutnant Heinrich Schmetz (who was to be awarded the Knight's Cross, and later go on to command the group), struck the 40,000-tonne (39,368-ton) battleship *Roma* amidships at a terminal velocity of about 330 metres (1080 feet) per second, punching straight through her bottom to explode beneath the ship. A second hit her just forward of the bridge, where her

armoured deck slowed it down fractionally, so that it exploded in the forward magazine beneath. She broke in two and sank within 40 minutes, carrying 1255 men down with her, including the commanding admiral, Bergamini. Her sister-ship the *Italia* was also hit by a missile which passed through the deck and side just forward of 'A' turret (ie, the most forward turret) before exploding in the sea. She took in 800 tonnes (787 tons) of water, but managed to make Malta, though she played no further part in the war.

More successes followed. On 11 September, the 10,000 tonne (9842-ton) American cruiser USS *Savannah* was disabled, as, two days later, was HMS *Uganda* (8500 tonnes; 8365 tons). Better still was the attack Jope himself carried out on the 33,000-tonne (32,478-ton) British battleship HMS *Warspite*, which was giving fire support off the Salerno beaches. The missile hit the *Warspite* amidships, and penetrated six decks before exploding against the bottom of the ship, blowing a large hole in her. She took in a total of 5000 tonnes (4921 tons) of water, lost steam (and thus all power, both to the ship herself and to all her systems), and had to be taken in tow. She reached Malta but was out of action for the next 12 months. The British

cruiser HMS *Spartan* and the destroyer HMS *Janus* were also sunk by X-1s, and the American cruiser USS *Philadelphia* was badly damaged.

THE HENSCHEL Hs 293

The Ruhrstahl X-1 development programme began at around the same time that Wagner's team at Henschel began work on the Hs 293. Surprisingly, development took longer, but it proved to be much simpler to train aircrew to 'fly' the bomb than the missile, and the two were eventually deployed together. Initially, the RLM had tried to persuade Henschel to produce a missile which levelled out just above the water some distance before reaching the target, and another which would actually submerge and act like a conventional torpedo, but the company refused on the grounds that such a course would be too ambitious, since there was no experience on which to draw. Instead, it put forward the concept of a straightforward guided glider bomb,

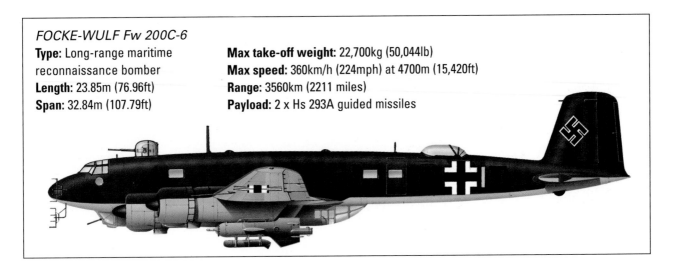

FOCKE-WULF Fw 200C-6
Type: Long-range maritime reconnaissance bomber
Length: 23.85m (76.96ft)
Span: 32.84m (107.79ft)

Max take-off weight: 22,700kg (50,044lb)
Max speed: 360km/h (224mph) at 4700m (15,420ft)
Range: 3560km (2211 miles)
Payload: 2 x Hs 293A guided missiles

unpowered but with aerodynamic properties, and the RLM agreed. The first experimental version, with no warhead, was tested in the spring of 1940, and by the end of the year a variant with a rocket motor, which allowed launch at 400m (1315ft) instead of the 1000m (3280ft) previously required, had been flown successfully, and plans for a production version of the latter were going ahead.

10 SECONDS OF THRUST

The Hs 293A-1 was built up from the nose and body sections of an SC (Sprengbombe Cylindrisch) 500 thin-walled bomb, with an elongated rear section tapering in the vertical plane, which extended above and below the body unequally to form small dorsal and larger ventral fins, carrying the guidance system. Short symmetrical wings with conventional ailerons were mounted where the bomb and tail section joined, and a tailplane with an equally conventional elevator was mounted just above their plane, where it would operate in clear air. The ailerons were actuated by electromagnets; the elevator by an electric motor and worm screw. The rocket motor – a liquid-propellant Walter 109-507B, using T-Stoff and Z-Stoff held in pressurised tanks – was underslung beneath the fuselage in a pod; it gave only 600kg (1300lb) of thrust for 10 seconds, but that was enough to propel the missile well ahead of the aircraft to a point where the bomb aimer could see it. This had been a recurring problem with the X-1, and one which could only be solved by the pilot of the launch aircraft throttling back and lowering his flaps until the aircraft almost stalled, which made him very vulnerable indeed.

The flight profile of the Hs 293 was quite different from that of the X-1. It was normally released at between 400m (1315ft) and 2000m (6560ft), and

Above: One of the German aircraft equipped to employ the Hs 293 rocket-propelled guided bomb was the long-range Focke-Wulf Fw 200 'Condor'. Two missiles could be carried, under the outboard engine nacelles.

between 3.5km (2.2 miles) and 18km (11 miles) short of the target. The terminal velocity varied between 435km/h (270mph) and 900km/h (560mph) depending on the altitude from which it had been released. Control, as always, was by joystick and radio link, on the Kehl/Strassburg system, but wire linkage was soon proposed and implemented, this time using a duplex bobbin system, with the wire being paid out from aircraft and missile simultaneously, giving a maximum range of 30km (18.7 miles). As with the X-1, flares in the tail – which were exchanged for small battery-powered lamps for night operations – allowed the bomb-aimer to keep track of the missile in flight.

A version of the basic weapon, with an extended nose to contain a television camera, was developed as the Hs 293D. The television equipment was developed by Fernseh GmbH in collaboration with the *Reichspost-Forschungsanstalt*. It was a vertical raster-scan 224-line system operating at 50Hz. Under ideal (laboratory) conditions, with its inventors to operate it, the system worked adequately enough, but under operational conditions it was much less successful and was finally abandoned. Such technology was not yet fully understood, and it was to be many years before it was perfected in weapons such as the American AGM-65 'Maverick' and the Anglo-French 'Martel' of the 1980s.

Other Hs 293 variants included the Hs 293H, which was discussed above in the context of air-to-air missiles, and the delta-winged, tailless (and stillborn) Hs 293F. It is unclear how many Hs 293s of all types

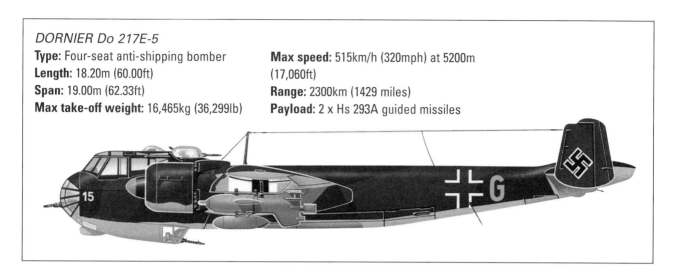

DORNIER Do 217E-5
Type: Four-seat anti-shipping bomber
Length: 18.20m (60.00ft)
Span: 19.00m (62.33ft)
Max take-off weight: 16,465kg (36,299lb)

Max speed: 515km/h (320mph) at 5200m
(17,060ft)
Range: 2300km (1429 miles)
Payload: 2 x Hs 293A guided missiles

were manufactured, but educated guesses put the number at perhaps 1500, many of which were expended in the long testing and training programme.

THE HS 293 IN ACTION

II Gruppe of Kampfgeschwader 100, flying Hs 293A-equipped Do 217E-5s out of Cognac under Hauptmann Heinz Molinus, was the first unit to go into

Above: Somewhat more successful than the Fw 200 was the Dornier Do 217E-5, which also carried two Hs 293As under its wings. It was one of these aircraft, of II/KG 100, which scored the first success with the new weapon.

Below: The bomb-aimer needed to keep the Hs 293 in sight all the way to the target, and for this purpose a multi-tube flare unit was attached to the bomb's tail.

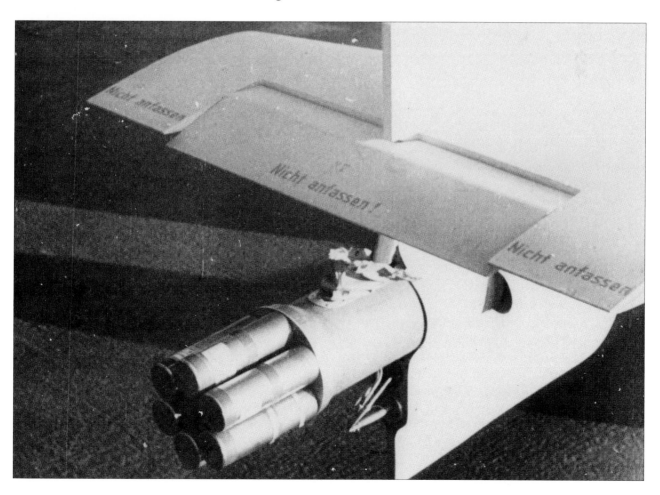

Above: The bomb-aimer controlled the Hs 293 using a two-axis joystick which transmitted signals either by radio or over wires. This installation is in an He 111H-12.

action armed with guided air-to-surface missiles, on 25 August 1943, against warships hunting German submarines in the Bay of Biscay. The first-ever kill with a guided missile came on 27 August, when one scored a direct hit on the 1270-tonne (1250-ton) sloop (ie, corvette) HMS *Egret*, detonating the ammunition in her after magazine and blowing her to pieces with the loss of 222 lives. In fact, II/KG100 later moved to Istres, near Marseilles, and II/KG40, equipped with He 177A-5s, replaced it on the Atlantic coast. Besides the *Egret*, Hs 293s accounted for five destroyers and a number of merchant ships before the Allies found a way to combat them using a set of defensive tactics which included jamming the radio control signals and targeting the launch aircraft during the vulnerable control phase, when they had to fly straight and level at reduced speed. These defensive tactics made the missions very costly. On 23 November, II/KG40 lost half its entire strength while attacking a well-protected convoy off the Algerian coast. Hs 293s were last used in action, with some success, against Red Army forces crossing the River Oder in April 1945, when they went into action with 'Mistel' (qv) piggyback hybrid aircraft.

THE BLOHM & VOSS ASMS

Blohm & Voss reacted to the RLM's requirement for a sea-skimming missile with a proposal for a guided glider bomb. This incorporated a rocket motor which was only ignited by tripping a 2m- (6.5ft-) long lever hanging from its underside when the bomb came to the end of its descent. It was an ingenious solution, but proved to be unworkable. The length of time available to initiate the rocket motor was just insufficient, and the prototypes simply ploughed into the sea. Rather better conceived was the Bv 246 'Hagelkorn' ('Hailstone'), which was a pure glider and was intended specifically to attack radio stations transmitting navigational signals to RAF bombers by homing in on their very signals. The Bv 246 was a simple aerodynamic shape with a cruciform empennage incorporating a vertical control surface, and high aspect-ratio wings designed to give it a shallow glide angle (1:25, or barely 4 degrees) and thus a long range after launch. Released at 10,500m (34,450ft), it had a range of 210km (130 miles). The original proposal was made in 1942, but there was little official interest despite the fact that the RAF had already begun to use radio as a navigational aid. It was December 1943 before 'Hagelkorn' was ordered into production and it was cancelled two months later in the February 1944 austerity drive, by which time hundreds had been built. These missiles were gradually expended in a protracted low-priority test programme which lasted until January 1945. With an all-up weight of 730kg (1600lb), of which 435kg (960lb) was warhead, it was light enough to be deployed by an Fw 190.

FLYING TORPEDOES

The RLM did not give up its search for an air-to-sub-surface weapon, and Henschel responded eventually with a variety of designs for what we may regard as guided air-launched torpedoes. The simplest of these

Below: The Blohm & Voss Bv 143 was a rocket-assisted glider bomb, the powerplant of which was ignited only when the projectile had come within 2m (6.5ft) of the surface of the sea.

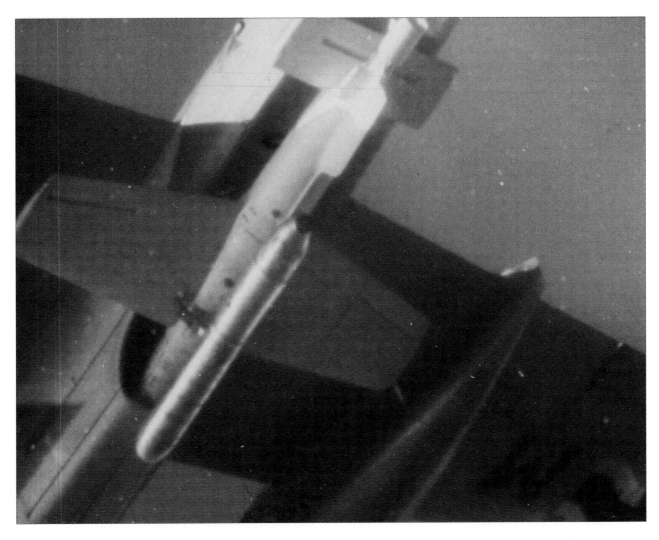

Above: The Dornier Do 217 was the aircraft of choice for the deployment of the Henschel Hs 294 anti-ship missile. Perhaps 1450 of these sophisticated guided missiles were ordered but few were completed.

Below: This sequence shows a launch of an Hs 294 which went disastrously wrong. Having disengaged from the parent Do 217 aircraft, the missile then collided with the bomber, slicing off a tail fin.

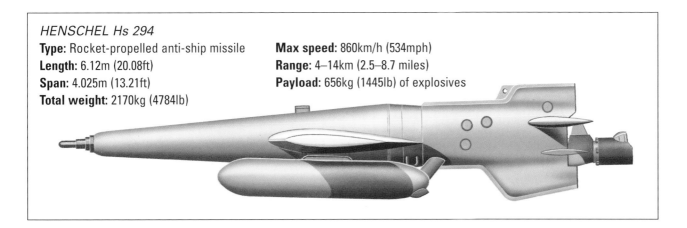

HENSCHEL Hs 294
Type: Rocket-propelled anti-ship missile
Length: 6.12m (20.08ft)
Span: 4.025m (13.21ft)
Total weight: 2170kg (4784lb)
Max speed: 860km/h (534mph)
Range: 4–14km (2.5–8.7 miles)
Payload: 656kg (1445lb) of explosives

was a version of the Hs 293, and from that, in 1943, sprang the larger and more powerful Hs 294, intended to be used to attack armoured ships. Two versions were produced in prototype form, one with radio guidance, the other with a wire command link.

The Hs 294 was essentially of the same form as the air-to-surface missile, with the addition of a long, tapered nose cone and a second rocket unit. It was to be flown into the sea at a shallow angle (optimum 22 degrees); the wings and the rear fuselage were mounted so that they would break away on hitting the water, and the warhead, with its 656kg (1445lb) explosive charge, would then be free to travel in a parabolic path, induced by the form of its upper surface, for up to 45m (150ft), self-destructing if it had not found its target. It is believed that a total of around 1450 were ordered, but few were produced.

The Hs 294 was followed by a rather more ambitious project known as the GT 1200, which certainly did not get past the prototype stage. GT 1200 was to have been an unpowered glider, with the guidance

Above: The Hs 294 was intended to enter the water cleanly some way from its target and strike it below the waterline, where it was at its most vulnerable.

package of the Hs 293, but without a rocket motor to assist its launch. Instead, the rocket motor, a standard Schmidding solid-fuel unit, was to have been used only during the last phase of its deployment, underwater, when, shorn of its wings and 'fuselage' extension, it became an otherwise conventional torpedo, steered by small rudders on its cruciform rear-mounted fins. There is no indication of how the missile was to have been guided during its run through the water. Henschel's last foray into the field of air-launched submarine weapons was to have been a supersonic missile known as the 'Zitterrochen' ('Torpedo Fish'), its triangular planform wings incorporating 'Wagner bars' – simply spoilers moved to the wing trailing edge – instead of ailerons. The project never got off the ground, but the control system found its way into the Hs 117 'Schmetterling' and the Hs 298.

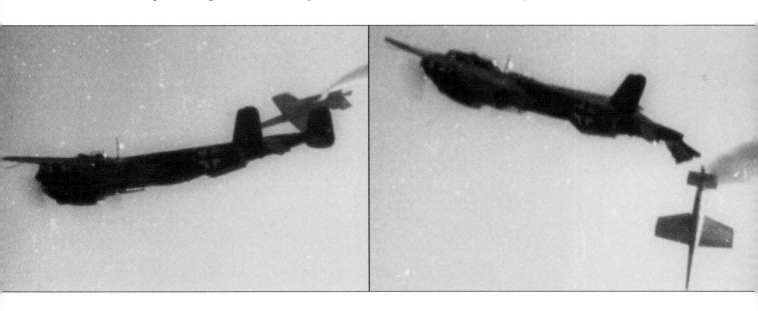

Surface-to-Air Missiles

In parallel with the programmes to develop air-to-air and air-to-surface missiles, German scientists and engineers also strove to produce guided surface-to-air missiles (SAMs). Work first began in 1941, but yet again, progress was overtaken by events; the first usable missiles were due to go into service in mid-1945, but by then the war was already over.

Finding ways to defeat the Allied bomber formations which pounded the Reich preoccupied the Luftwaffe and the RLM alike. As a result, a number of teams were at work developing new weapons. Most important amongst these were the more-or-less successful jet and rocket-powered aircraft we have already discussed. However, much energy and resources went into developing surface-to-air missiles (SAMs) too, amongst the most significant of which

Above: The Messerschmitt 'Enzian' was made largely of plywood and flew at subsonic speeds.

Left: Like the 'Enzian', the 'Wasserfall' relied on blast effects; its warhead was detonated by an artillery fuze.

were the Henschel Hs 117 'Schmetterling' ('Butterfly'), the Messerschmitt 'Enzian' ('Gentian'), the Rheinmetall-Borsig 'Rheintochter' ('Rhine Maiden'), and the EMW 'Wasserfall' ('Waterfall') – all of which had a guidance system – and the EMW 'Taifun' ('Typhoon'), which was unguided.

THE HENSCHEL Hs 117 'SCHMETTERLING'

The earliest of the projects was for a subsonic short-to-medium-range missile which was radio controlled by an operator on the ground. Henschel first began work on the project in 1941, alongside a number of unguided flak rockets, and two years later was ordered to develop it as the Hs 117. With stubby swept-back wings and a cruciform tail, the Hs 117

'Schmetterling' was controlled like an aircraft, with solenoid-operated 'Wagner bars' rather than conventional ailerons on the trailing edges of the wings and tailplane. It appeared somewhat unbalanced, having a bifurcated nose, with the starboard cone elongated to form a warhead extension and the port cone finishing in a small airscrew driving a generator. Launch power was supplied by a pair of external solid-fuel motors, one above and one below the fuselage, which gave 1750kg (3850lb) of boost for four seconds, accelerating the missile to 1100km/h (680mph) before falling away and igniting the sustainer motor. The motor was to have been either a BMW 109-558 or a Walter 109-729, both of which used liquid fuel – R-Stoff or 'Tonka', a composite self-igniting fuel, with SV-Stoff (concentrated nitric acid) as an oxidizer in the former; SV-Stoff and Br-Stoff (low-octane petrol), with an alcohol igniter, in the latter.

LAUNCHING THE 'SCHMETTERLING'

At 4.3m (14ft) long and weighing a total of 420kg (925lb) including the solid-fuel motors, the 'Schmetterling' was launched from a modified anti-aircraft gun mounting, azimuth and elevation being approximately pre-set manually by the launch crew.

Once in flight, a flare in the tail was ignited, and the controller observed its progress through a telescope, correcting by radio using the Kehl/Strassburg system codenamed 'Parsival' (FuG203/230), which was also widely used for other operator-guided missiles, employing four separate radio frequencies, two for the horizontal axis and two for the vertical. Control was by a simple joystick. A fifth radio frequency was used to detonate the 25kg (55lb) warhead, which relied on blast rather than fragmentation, on command, though proximitiy and time delay fuzes were also developed. The effective range was 16km (10 miles) and the ceiling was 11,000m (36,000ft). In blind conditions it was hoped to employ the Mannheim-Reise/'Rheingold' radar system, which worked something like the Würzburg fighter control system, one set tracking the target, the other the missile; the operator would use the joystick as before, but would now be observing dots on a cathode ray tube, and trying to keep them superimposed. Later, it was hoped, corrections would be applied automatically.

Below: The Henschel Hs 117 'Schmetterling' was the first attempt by Germany to develop a surface-to-air missile; it was for use against low- and medium-altitude intruders.

HENSCHEL Hs 117
Type: Rocket-propelled surface-to-air missile
Length: 4.29m (14ft)
Diameter: 350mm (13.77in)

Launch weight: 445kg (981lb)
Max range: 32km (20 miles)
Warhead: 25kg (55lb) of high explosive

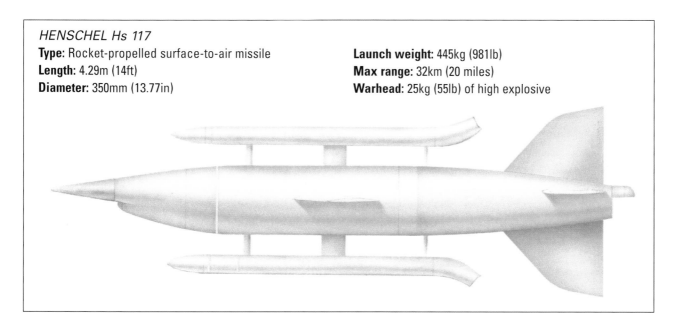

Testing of the 'Schmetterling' began in May 1944, and by September, 22 launches had been made, some of them of a variant intended as an air-to-air missile, the Hs 117H (qv). The success rate was good enough that the missile was ordered into production in December, with first deliveries – 150 units per month – to take place in March 1945, rising to 3000 per month by November. This was hopelessly optimistic, of course, at a time when industrial output in Germany was failing fast, and no missile was ever produced for operational use.

THE MESSERSCHMITT 'ENZIAN'

Messerschmitt's proposal resembled an unmanned version of the Me 163 'Komet', with the same stubby body and wings and the twin ventral/dorsal tail fins. It was considerably heavier than the 'Schmetterling' at 1800kg (3970lb), had a 300kg (660lb) warhead, and was designed to operate at up to 12,000m (41,000ft) or out to a range of 24.5km (15.25 miles) at lower levels. One most important feature of the 'Enzian' was the fact that its airframe was to be constructed of moulded plywood, a material Germany had in abundance, and this was almost – but not quite – enough to give it sufficient official approval points to actually see it into production, especially since it used technology which was well understood.

The 'Enzian', originally the Flak Rakete 1, was designed from June 1943 by a team led by Hermann Wurster at Messerschmitt's R&D headquarters at Oberammergau, with prototypes to be produced at Augsburg and serial airframe manufacture to be carried out at Holzbau Kissing AG, in nearby Sonthofen.

Above: The Henschel Hs 117 'Schmetterling' surface-to-air missile. The Hs 117 was also produced in an air-to-air version which lacked the SAM's external boosters.

Like the 'Komet', it had a circular-section fuselage, 0.9m (3ft) in maximum diameter; it also had ventral and dorsal fins and mid-mounted swept-back wings with full-width elevons, which operated in unison or independently and thus obviated the need for a rudder. Launch power was provided by four Schmidding 109-533 diglycol-fuelled rockets, the same as that employed for the 'Schmetterling', which gave a combined thrust of 7000kg (15,400lb) for four seconds and were then jettisoned. The launch platform consisted of 6.8m (22.25ft) rails on a modified 8.8cm anti-aircraft gun mounting, which could of course be trained in azimuth and elevation. The sustainer rocket was to have been a Walter R1-210B, using SV-Stoff and Br-Stoff as its fuel, delivered to the combustion chamber by a pair of steam-driven turbo-pumps as employed in the A4. About 15 of these motors are thought to have been produced, and they were used to test the prototype missiles, but for the production version a simplified motor was designed by Drs Konrad and Beck of the *Deutsches Versuchsanstalt für Kraftfahrzeug- und Fahrzeugmotoren* (DVK – the German Aviation Propulsion Experimental Establishment), which used S-Stoff and Visol delivered by compressed air, and in its final form gave the slightly higher performance figures of 2500kg (5510lb) of thrust falling to 1500kg (3300lb) by the end of its 56-second burn time. The reducing thrust ensured that the missile did not exceed its maximum

Mach number and become unstable. Guidance was exactly the same as for the 'Schmetterling' and the same sort of proximity fuze was to have been used.

Perhaps 60 'Enzian' missiles were constructed, of which 38 were tested, beginning in April 1944. The first examples fared badly because the designers had not grasped the importance of aligning the missile's axial centre of gravity and thrust lines, but that was cured, and later tests proved successful. The 'Enzian' fell foul of the general deterioration in manufacturing capacity, and as there was concern at RLM that it was detracting from the production of Me 163s and Me 262s, in January 1945 the project was axed.

THE RHEINMETALL-BORSIG MISSILES

Although successful with its unguided 'Rheinbote' bombardment missiles, Rheinmetall-Borsig achieved less with its surface-to-air missiles. The company's first foray into the field was a winged missile called the 'Hecht' ('Pike'), which seems to have been no more than a design and concept-proving exercise; several are known to have been air-dropped, both in powered and unpowered forms. Work on it stopped in 1941, when the 'Feuerlilie' project was initiated; it

seems that this, too, was to have been purely a research programme, but the RLM insisted that it be adaptable to use as an anti-aircraft rocket, should that prove necessary. Even though there is no evidence that that step was taken, and the missile was unguided, we may include it here in passing.

The 'Firelily' was to have a streamlined cylindrical fuselage with rear-mounted swept-back wings terminating in small symmetrical fins. It was to have been produced in a number of versions of different fuselage diameter, the most important of which were the F25 and the F55, and was to have been propelled by solid-fuel rockets which the company already had in production as take-off assistance units (RATO) for gliders and heavily-loaded transport aircraft, though there was also a plan to produce a supersonic version of the 55cm missile, with simple fins in place of the wing assembly, to be powered by a Konrad-designed liquid-fuel rocket. The 'Firelily' project continued

Below: In looks, 'Enzian' resembled the Messerschmitt Me 163 'Komet' rocket plane. Like all liquid-fuelled rockets, most of the internal space of the 'Enzian' was taken up with fuel tanks.

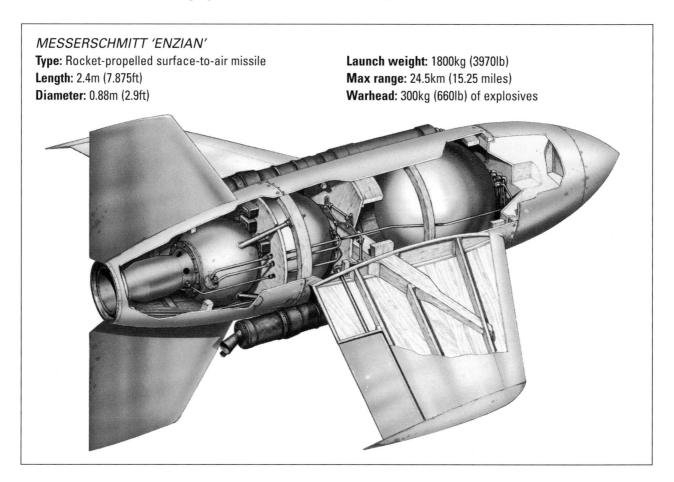

MESSERSCHMITT 'ENZIAN'
Type: Rocket-propelled surface-to-air missile
Length: 2.4m (7.875ft)
Diameter: 0.88m (2.9ft)

Launch weight: 1800kg (3970lb)
Max range: 24.5km (15.25 miles)
Warhead: 300kg (660lb) of explosives

Above: Rheinmetall was better known for its artillery pieces, but its 'Rheintochter' SAM was an ambitious design intended to fly at up to 1300km/h (800mph).

until early 1945, but it seems clear that no attempt was ever made to utilise the missiles as weapons. Several F25s were manufactured and were tested at Peenemünde-West and at the company's own proving grounds at Leba, but certainly no operational variant was ever produced. Perhaps six F55s were produced; one was tested successfully at Leba, and two were sent to Peenemünde, where the one went out of control when launched.

The 'Rhine Maiden' was an entirely different matter. It was conceived from the outset as an anti-aircraft missile. It was an ambitious design incorporating two stages: the cylindrical first stage housed nothing but solid-fuel booster rockets, and had four fixed, swept-back fins with bracing struts between them, which acted simply as stabilisers, being jettisoned on burn-out; the second stage, also cylindrical, tapered to a point at the nose and slightly at the tail, and had six fixed fins mounted about two-thirds the way back from the nose, and four small rounded steering surfaces – canards, in effect – at the nose itself, which were actuated by servos to guide the rocket in flight. Unusually, the warhead was situated in the rear of the rocket, behind the fins and motor unit, the six venturi of which were positioned between the fins, angled out, which also worked to help stabilise the missile in flight. 'Rheintochter I' was intended to reach speeds of almost 1300km/h (800mph), and carry a 100–150kg (220–330lb) warload to 40km (25 miles) and 6000m (19,700ft). The missile had a lengthy

development period. The contract was signed in November 1942, but by late 1944 only a relatively small number – perhaps 50 – had been launched, less than half of which carried guidance equipment that was essentially similar to that incorporated in 'Schmetterling' and 'Enzian' and in the more successful guided glide bombs. At the year's end, the project was abandoned, the missile never having come close to reaching its design altitude.

It seems that the development team had known all along that the RATO units would never produce the required performance, and had planned to power the production version of the missile, known as 'Rheintochter III', with a version of the same Konrad-designed liquid-fuel rocket which was to go into the supersonic 'Feuerlilie', though a version with a much-enlarged solid-fuel rocket was also proposed. This was, in fact, the only version of the 'Rheintochter III' ever tested.

THE EMW 'WASSERFALL'

Although Wernher von Braun worked for the German Army, and anti-aircraft defences were the responsibility of the Luftwaffe, EMW was ordered to produce an anti-aircraft guided missile. Most of the necessary work had already been done in developing the A4,

Above: The 'Rheintochter' 1 on its launch ramp. Guidance was provided by the small vanes at the nose, which were controlled from the ground via radio signals.

and the chief difference between 'Wasserfall' – as the surface-to-air missile was known – and the A4 was to be in its propulsion plant. From the outset it was clear that the operational requirements for the two rockets were quite different. Whereas A4 could be fuelled as and when required, in a more or less leisurely fashion, and fired when it was ready, the SAM would be required to be held at instant readiness, perhaps for months, and this was simply not practical if a cryogenic propellant like liquid oxygen was employed. Instead, it would be fuelled by Salbei (90 per cent nitric acid, 10 per cent sulphuric acid to inhibit corrosion) and a type of Visol, the fuel – which ignited spontaneously on being combined – being delivered to the combustion chamber by pressurising the propellant tanks with inert nitrogen, rather than by using cumbersome high-pressure steam turbines. Because the two components of the fuel reacted so violently, pre-launch and launch-time safety procedures very important, and there was an elaborate system of interlocks involving metal membranes which would rupture only in predetermined circumstances.

'Wasserfall' was about half the length of the A4, at 7.84m (25.7ft), and weighed 3500kg (7720lb) all-up, as opposed to 12,900kg (28,440lb), but it was still by far the biggest of all the German surface-to-air

weapons, even though its warhead was smaller, at 235kg (520lb), than that of the 'Enzian'. It was very similar in shape to the bigger missile, but unlike the A4 it had four stabilising fins located about one third the way back from the nose.

35 TEST LAUNCHES

'Wasserfall' was designed to operate at greater range and altitude than the other SAMs. Its 8000kg- (17,630lb-) thrust engine burned for 40 seconds and gave it a range of up to 50km (30 miles) and an altitude of 20,000m (65,000ft), even though the latter was far higher than any aircraft attained. Its guidance system was manual and ground-based, with course corrections transmitted to the rocket by radio signals, but since it was launched vertically, it also carried the A4's basic inertial guidance system, to point it in the approximate direction of the target. It is difficult to imagine visual tracking and control being at all effective at anything like extreme range and altitude, and given its high launch speed, guiding it manually at all, whether through a sighting telescope or by superimposing dots on an oscilloscope, generated by tracking radars, must have presented problems. The first successful launch occurred at Peenemünde on 29 February 1944, and it is believed that about 35 test launches were made in total. Series production was to have been at the biggest underground factory of them all, Bleichrode, but in the event even the factory itself had not been built when the war ended in May 1945.

THE UNGUIDED 'TAIFUN'

By mid-1944, there were many in Germany who advocated cancelling the offensive weapons development programme completely in order to concentrate on developing more effective defensive measures, but of course Adolf Hitler was not one of them, and what he said still went. The 'Aggregat' programme certainly got priority at Peenemünde, and since the same team was working on 'Wasserfall', that inevitably meant that the latter lost out because resources were not available. The A4 got into production, while 'Wasserfall' did not. In fact, there was not even a clear consensus in favour of 'Wasserfall', or even general acceptance of its desirability. Some at EMW even advocated scrapping 'Wasserfall' (on the grounds that it would never work successfully without an automatic guidance system) and concentrating on a simpler, unguided flak rocket.

A design for just such a missile was put forward by the Range Officer at Peenemünde, an engineer named Scheufeln, and was – perhaps somewhat surprisingly, considering all the other demands being put on that establishment – ordered into development in September 1944 as the 'Taifun' ('Typhoon'). The first examples used solid-fuel motors, but it soon became apparent that they would not reach the desired height (the 'Rheintochter' development team was having the same problem, we may recall), and liquid propellants Salbei and Visol were used instead. They were stored in concentric cylindrical tanks, which made up the body of the missile, and forced into the combustion chamber by nitrogen under pressure, a cunningly designed valve ensuring that initially there was a fuel-rich mixture in the chamber which allowed pressure there to build up slowly and evenly (relatively speaking since the delay between triggering and firing was one tenth of a second). This was to prove most effective, and was to make 'Taifun' surprisingly accurate even at high altitude, which meant that the warhead could be fitted with a contact or graze fuze, and needed to be no bigger than a conventional anti-aircraft artillery shell of 0.5kg (1.1lb).

Overall, the missile was 1.93m (6.3ft) long and 100mm (4in) in diameter. It weighed 21kg (46lb) before launch, and reached a height of 15,000m (49,210ft) before falling back to earth, with a maximum velocity of 3600km/h (2235mph). It went into limited production at Peenemünde in January 1945, and an estimated 600 were completed, along with a small number of launchers (which were based, once again, on the mounting of the 8.8cm FlaK 37). Unit cost would have been very low and, at RM25, less than a third of the price of a rifle. There is no clear indication whether it was ever used operationally, and no evidence to suggest that it ever brought down an aircraft, though that is certainly possible, since to the target's crew, it would have appeared that the aircraft had been hit by conventional anti-aircraft fire.

Below: The 'Wasserfall' was essentially a scaled-down A4 (V2) rocket; it weighed 3.5 tonnes (3.4 tons) and reached an altitude of 20km (12.5 miles).

CHAPTER NINE

Artillery

By the end of the nineteenth century, artillery pieces had already reached a very high standard of sophistication, being able to hit small targets at ranges of 25km (15.5 miles) and more. There was really very little left for gunmakers to do save to make them bigger and yet bigger still, and that is just what the likes of Krupp, long recognised as masters in the field, did.

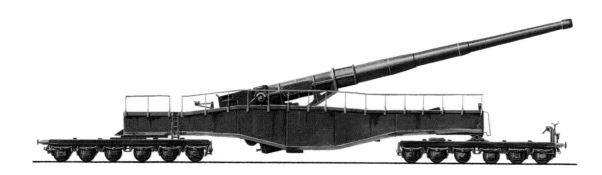

Germany had some success with ultra-long-range artillery during World War I, notably with the so-called 'Paris Gun'. The Imperial German Navy, which constructed and manned them, called them the 'Kaiser Wilhelm Geschütz', and they were used sporadically from March to July 1918 during the massive and so nearly effective German counter-attack in Picardy to bombard the French capital from the region north of Soissons over 100km (60 miles) away. They were 38cm (15in) naval guns, as mounted aboard the battleships of the day, sleeved down to 21cm (8.25in) with liners whose rifling consisted of

Above: The K5 (E), a 28cm gun mounted on a railway car, was perhaps the most successful of the 'superguns'.

Left: This 38cm gun, its barrel 45 calibres long, was derived from a weapon designed for battleships.

deep grooves within which lugs on the shell located, a method first adopted in the early days of the development of the rifled gun in the 1840s. This same method was to be employed in the very long-range artillery pieces developed in Germany for use in World War II – the K5 battlefield weapons and the 'strategic' K12, built to fire on England from the French coast – though the shells of these guns were rather more sophisticated. Heavily over-charged, they projected their shell into the stratosphere where, meeting little air resistance, it could extend its trajectory considerably. The use of a far heavier charge than the gun had ever been designed to employ soon caused the barrel to wear out – it seems that 25cm (10in) of rifling was destroyed with every round fired, and that a barrel's life was just 50 rounds in consequence – and it then had to be rebored or relined. The Paris Guns, with three mountings and seven barrels, which were employed serially, fired just 303 rounds towards Paris, slightly more than half of which (183) actually landed within its boundaries, killing 256 and wounding 620. These results made the entire project highly cost-ineffective, except in propaganda terms.

Though these first-generation ultra-long-range guns were to enjoy only limited success, they did, albeit imperfectly, solve the problem of how to bombard high-value area targets with relative impunity from outside the range of counter-battery fire. In more modern times they would be sickeningly vulnerable to air attack, since they presented big targets, were hard to conceal, and impossible to move at very short notice, but in 1918, despite a huge campaign to locate them, they were never found. By the time the Allies overran the Forest of Crépy, where they were located, there was no sign of them left save their concrete emplacements. Another problem – and many said a more pressing one – remained: how to subdue organised defensive positions like the modern fortresses of the Maginot Line, which ran down the French-German border, in the shortest possible time. For this, a

Below: Krupp made two massive 80cm guns, 'Gustav' and 'Dora'; they fired a 7.1-tonne (7-ton) anti-concrete shell 32km (20 miles) but required a crew of 2000.

task which was to be undertaken at shorter range, an approach which can almost be characterised as 'brute force and ignorance' was all that was necessary, and the guns in question were no more than straightforward developments of the siege guns which were some of the first weapons deployed in 1914.

'BIG BERTHA'

In August of that year, the German Army advanced through Belgium in order to execute the Schlieffen Plan, sweeping through northern France to take Paris from the northwest and thus avoid the hardened defensive positions which dominated the approach routes from Germany. For the most part, and exactly as expected, they met little resistance, except from the forts surrounding the vital city of Liège, and to subdue these, they called up the big guns, the 42cm (16.5in) siege howitzers. The operation took longer than envisaged, but in the end 'Big Bertha' and her sisters, as the British came to call the guns, prevailed. They were not always to be so successful, however; they were later taken to Verdun and used against the fortress complex there to much less effect. These guns were enormous, by any definition – after all, they fired a shell which stood almost as high as a man, and weighed in excess of a ton – and moving them was no

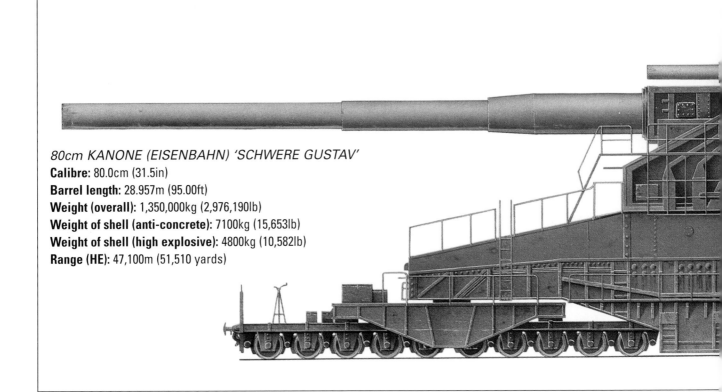

80cm KANONE (EISENBAHN) 'SCHWERE GUSTAV'
Calibre: 80.0cm (31.5in)
Barrel length: 28.957m (95.00ft)
Weight (overall): 1,350,000kg (2,976,190lb)
Weight of shell (anti-concrete): 7100kg (15,653lb)
Weight of shell (high explosive): 4800kg (10,582lb)
Range (HE): 47,100m (51,510 yards)

simple matter. In around 20 hours, they broke down into 172 pieces, and could then be transported on 12 railway wagons. Not surprisingly (especially since it was often necessary to construct railway lines first) moving such monsters in and out of position was a major operation, but there was no alternative, and the sheer size of the guns was one of the most important motives for the German Army's interest in much more mobile rocketry. It had been a limiting factor in World War I, and was to remain one in World War II.

Bertha was the daughter of Friedrich Alfred Krupp, son of the founder of the company, and the wife of Gustav von Bohlen und Halbach. 'Big Bertha' had been manufactured by Krupp, and it was to the Essen-based company that the *Heereswaffenamt* (HWA – the German Army's weapons development and procurement office) turned in the mid-1930s when it realised that while the 'new' strategy of war, the Blitzkrieg, once more placed the emphasis on movement, there would still inevitably be fortresses to subdue. In response to the HWA's request, Krupp's engineers produced outline proposals for three guns, of 70, 80 and 100cm calibre. The most realistic of those was the 80cm gun, which would fire a projectile weighing up to 7.11 tonnes (7 tons) to a range of around 32km (20 miles). It would weigh around 1370 tonnes (1350 tons) and require a crew approaching 2000 strong. It would be mobile, but only in the loosest possible sense, for it would take around three weeks to dismantle it and the same to put it together again, and would need twin railway tracks for the whole of its journey, with an additional pair of tracks for the cranes required for assembly and disassembly.

'GUSTAV' AND 'DORA'

Nothing more on the subject was heard from the HWA, and Krupp's technicians went back to the more realistic task of developing the K5 and K12. There the matter may have rested, but in 1936, Hitler visited the establishment and began asking about the possibility of developing guns to defeat the Maginot Line. Gustav Krupp told him of the 80cm gun project, and as soon as the visit was concluded, well knowing Hitler's weakness for the gargantuan, Krupp had his staff draw up detailed plans. These were submitted to the HWA early in 1937, and the response was an order to construct three guns, work to start immediately and to be completed by 1940.

In the event, the barrels proved very difficult to manufacture, and Krupp missed the deadline by a considerable margin. By the time they were ready to proceed, the German Army had simply bypassed the

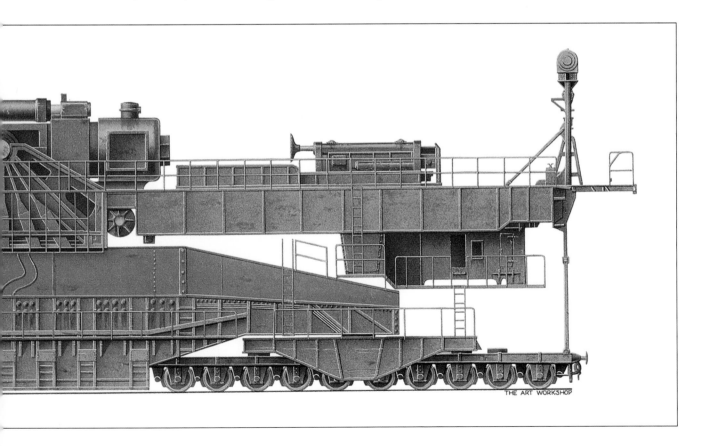

THE ART WORKSHOP

Above: The barrels of very large-calibre guns were transported dismounted. This barrel was captured by Allied forces at the war's end.

Maginot Line. With no suitable target immediately to hand, work slowed down, and it was the end of the year before the first barrel was completed, and 1941 before it was proofed. Only then was it worth setting to work on building the very complicated carriage, and that took the rest of the year. It was 1942 before the first complete gun was transported to the firing ranges at Rügenwald on the Baltic coast, assembled and tested, in the presence of Hitler himself. All went well and 'Gustav', as the gun had been christened, in honour of the company's Chairman, was presented to the nation with the company's compliments, to be followed almost immediately by 'Dora', named after the wife of the chief designer, Erich Muller.

THE BOMBARDMENT OF SEBASTOPOL

By 1942, the course of World War II had taken a drastic turn following Hitler's declaration of war on the Soviet Union. There may have been no worthwhile targets for 'Gustav' in Western Europe, but there were now plenty to the east. The gun was broken down into its components, they were loaded aboard their specially constructed railway flatcars, with the carriage base trundling along independently, occupying twin tracks, and the whole ensemble got underway for the Crimea. 'Gustav' was set up some 16km (10 miles) to the northeast of Sebastopol, which was still holding out, where it fired 48 rounds in all (including one which, most spectacularly, blew up an underground magazine) and played a significant part in the fall of the city, whereupon it was shipped back to Essen in order for the barrel to be relined. 'Dora' took its place, but it is doubtful whether it actually saw action, since the Red Army soon counter-attacked and surrounded the Germans, and by that time it had been safely evacuated. There are no substantiated reports of either gun having been used in anger again, though there are reports of 'Gustav' having seen action at Leningrad and 'Dora' having been sent to Warsaw to take part in the bombardment after the uprising in 1944. At the war's end, parts of 'Dora' were found near Leipzig, parts of 'Gustav' in Bavaria, and components of the third gun, which was never completed, in Essen. The project proved to be a very expensive exercise in futility: seven million Reichsmarks per gun, without the cost of the special trains needed to transport them and the manpower required both to manufacture and to operate them. There were various schemes put forward for improved versions on the original carriages. These included one in 52cm calibre to fire a 1.42-tonne (1.4-ton) shell to a range of about 113km (70 miles); one to fire a 38cm sabotted sub-calibre shell to over 145km (90 miles) and even to fire rocket-assisted projectiles to something like 193km (120 miles); and a smooth-bore version to fire a version of the fin-stabilised, dart-like projectile called the 'Peenemünde arrow shell' (*Peenemünde Pfeilgeschoss*), developed for the K5 gun (see below). None came to anything.

THE GERAT 041

The 'Gustav Gerät' guns were not the only fortress-smashers constructed for the German Army. Rather more satisfactory, and more practical, were the self-propelled 60cm howitzers developed by Rheinmetall as the Gerät 041, known unofficially as 'Karl', after General Karl Becker, whose brainchild they were. These were short-barrelled weapons, more like mortars than howitzers, with a maximum range of 4.5km (2.8 miles); they fired a 2.23-tonne (2.2-ton) shell specially designed to destroy reinforced-concrete structures such as blockhouses by burrowing into them for 2.5m (8.2ft) before exploding their 240kg (529lb) charge.

The complete ensemble weighed 124 tonnes (122 tons), and if the howitzers themselves were massive, the carriages upon which they rode were hardly less so at 11.3m (37ft) long, with full-length tracks with eight, and later 11, small roadwheels, each one independently sprung on a torsion bar. The vehicle could be jacked down to allow its hull to rest on the ground, thus avoiding the effects of recoil on the suspension. The recoil system itself was duplex: the gun recoiled

Below: Rheinmetall constructed six 60cm self-propelled mortars for the Wehrmacht. These 'fortress smashers' – this is 'Thor' – were used all along the Eastern Front.

within a cradle, which in turn recoiled along the chassis, controlled by hydro-pneumatic compensators. The vehicles were powered by 44.5-litre motors, although they were only expected to travel for short distances under their own power. For longer journeys they were loaded aboard specially built transporters or on railway cars. Six were manufactured, together with tracked, armoured ammunition carrier/loaders, and were issued to 628 Heavy Artillery Battalion (Motorised), which promptly named them 'Adam', 'Eve', 'Odin', 'Thor', 'Loki' and 'Ziu'. They first went into action at the Siege of Brest-Litovsk in June 1941, and were also present at Lvov and Sebastopol as well as elsewhere. In 1942, the Army asked for proposals to increase their range, and Rheinmetall's answer was to produce new barrels in 54cm calibre which fired 1250kg (2755lb) shells to a maximum range of about 10km (6.2 miles). From then on, the barrels seem to have been swapped to suit whatever ordnance there was available. Two were seized by American forces in Bavaria in 1945.

Above: The 60cm mortars fired a shell weighing 2.23 tonnes (2.2 tons), which was specially designed to drive deep into a fortification before exploding.

THE K5 GUNS

Also considerably more practical than 'Gustav' and 'Dora' were the K5 guns in 28cm calibre, which fired 255kg (565lb) shells out to a range of close to 64km (40 miles). A total of 28 of these were constructed between 1936 and 1945, and all were used most effectively in combat, the most famous probably being 'Anzio Annie', which was used to bombard the Anzio beachhead, and is now on display at the US Army's artillery proving grounds at Aberdeen, Maryland. Like the Paris Guns, the K5 employed deeply incised rifling – the 12 grooves were 7mm (0.25in) deep – and each shell had very precisely machined curved slots into which were inserted soft iron rails to form splines, matching the pattern in the barrel exactly, instead of the simple lugs or studs of the original. These guns too were mounted on railway cars, though unlike the 'Gustav Gerät', they were transportable largely intact, and could thus be put into and out of action much more quickly and easily. They were fully practical weapons, and the smaller 24cm K3, built by Rheinmetall, was perhaps better still, especially in its improved form, the Krupp-developed K4.

However, that did not prevent the development of projects to improve on these weapons. One of those was to produce a rocket-assisted projectile (RAP), which grew out of an attempt to develop a 15cm RAP for an existing gun. This proved to be much more practicable in the extra volume available. The shell was in two parts, the head containing the solid propellant, with a blast tube leading down to the base, surrounded by a conventional high-explosive filling. The propellant was ignited by a time fuze which detonated 19 seconds into the projectile's flight when it was approaching the apogee of its trajectory and boosted its velocity. The maximum range achieved on test was 86.5km (53.7 miles), and it was calculated that half the shells would land in an elongated target area around 3500m (11,482ft) long and 200m (656ft) wide, which was entirely acceptable given the nature of the likely targets.

The RAP, an accepted part of the artilleryman's arsenal only by the 1980s, was not the only new projectile developed for the K5 gun. Scientists at Pennemünde also became involved in the attempts to increase the K5's range, and came up with the *Pfeilgeschoss*, in this case a projectile 120mm (4.7in) in diameter, 1.8m (6ft) long, with four fins and a form of rudimentary sabot, which was little more than a three-part flange, 31cm (7.9in) in diameter, which was to be fired from a version of the gun with a smooth-bore barrel bored out to that same calibre. The sabot flange was discarded as soon as the projectile was in free flight. With a suitable propellant charge to take its trajectory well into the stratosphere, this projectile, which had a 25kg (55lb) explosive payload, reached a maximum range of almost 155km (95 miles). Development began as early as 1940, but with a low-grade priority it did not culminate until 1944. *Pfeilgeschossen* were issued, and seem to have been used in combat, albeit in small numbers, in

Below: Rheinmetall also built railway guns in 24cm calibre; this one is seen in northern France, firing at targets in Kent, across the English Channel.

1945. The projectile was the forerunner of the FSDS (fin-stabilised, discarding sabot) round, now in common use. The credit for the original idea is usually accorded to a French gun designer, Edgar Brandt, better known for the infantry mortars he developed; in the 1930s he produced a very effective 105mm/75mm projectile, which had very superior performance when fired from a 105mm gun with a standard charge.

THE 'CROSS-CHANNEL' GUN

Meanwhile, Krupp's engineers were also working on a 'brute force' solution to firing a projectile out to 80km (50 miles) or more by a simple process of refining the original design of the Paris Gun. The result was the K12, in 21cm calibre, which used the same rifling and shell-seating method as the K5, with the addition of a composite copper/asbestos/graphite band to improve its sealing within the tube and maximise the effect of the propellant charge. It was hoped that the use of soft iron splines rather than simple lugs would both cause them, and not the hardened molybnedum-steel of the barrel, to wear, and also spread the load of rotational acceleration, thus prolonging barrel life even in the presence of an abnormally large pro-

pellant charge. The first barrel was proofed in 1937 and the first complete gun, the K12(V), was tested in 1938 and declared serviceable in 1939. It fired a 107.5kg (237lb) shell out to a maximum range of 115km (71.5 miles) and the Army declared itself satisfied, for it was a greater distance than the Navy had achieved with the Paris Gun. Beating that record seems to have been a major incentive. However, it was less than perfect in operation. It had to be jacked up by 1m (3.3ft) into its firing position, so as to allow extra space for recoil, and then returned to the lower position for loading. Krupp was asked to devise an alternative mounting sub-frame and so produced a modified gun with strengthened hydraulic buffers as the K12 (N) in the summer of 1940. No more were ever constructed.

Mounting the gun presented problems of its own. To begin with, its barrel was 157 calibres long, well over three times the length of comparable naval guns, more than 33m (108ft) from breech to muzzle. This

Below: Two K5s were in action against Allied forces contained on the beachhead at Anzio for four months in 1944. One was captured and shipped back to the USA.

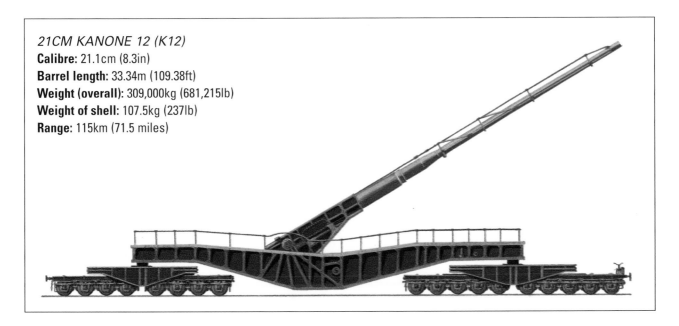

21CM KANONE 12 (K12)
Calibre: 21.1cm (8.3in)
Barrel length: 33.34m (109.38ft)
Weight (overall): 309,000kg (681,215lb)
Weight of shell: 107.5kg (237lb)
Range: 115km (71.5 miles)

meant that it distorted under its own weight and had to be very carefully braced. It also needed its trunnions to be very accurately located at the centre of balance, otherwise elevation would have been very difficult. The mount was in the form of an over-size railway car (more accurately, two railways cars); the main structure, with the trunnion supports and elevating machinery, was mounted on two sub-frames each of which, in turn, was mounted on a pair of bogies, two eight-wheeled units to the fore and two ten-wheeled units behind. For operational purposes it ran on a track section laid in an arc, and it was trained by running it backwards and forwards. The whole ensemble weighed 304.8 tonnes (300 tons) and was over 41m (135ft) long. It appears that the two guns were operational, with Eisenbahn Batterie 701, only for brief periods in late 1940 until early 1941, and they were directed at targets in Kent, particularly around Dover, from emplacements in the Pas de Calais. The greatest range attained seems to have been of the order of 90km (56 miles). One example was captured by Allied forces in Holland in 1945.

THE HIGH-PRESSURE PUMP

The K12 guns were not the only weapon developed with an eye to bombarding southern England with artillery fire, but the other project, the so-called 'High-pressure Pump', was much less conventional, and relied on a principle first demonstrated, albeit imperfectly, in the United States of America around 1885. It was the work of Lyman and Haskell, who reasoned that subsidiary propellant charges, spaced at intervals up the barrel of a gun in side-chambers and

Above: The 21cm K12 railway gun had the longest range of all the 'superguns' – around 115km (71.5 miles), depending on weather conditions.

ignited a micro-instant after a shell had travelled past on its way up the barrel, would provide a subsidiary propellant force and thus increase the muzzle velocity of the projectile. The result, when they built it on the instructions of the US Army's Chief of Ordnance, didn't much resemble an artillery piece as we know it. Firstly, the barrel had to be so long that it could not be supported save on the ground and had to be laid on an inclined ramp; and secondly, it had pairs of chambers, angled back at 45 degrees, let into it for much of its length. In the event, it didn't work: obturation was faulty, the flash from the original propellant charge bypassed the shell and ignited the subsidiary charges ahead of it, defeating the whole object of the exercise. Lyman and Haskell gave up, and the idea was consigned to the history books. It was apparently raised again in Britian, during World War I, but was turned down once more.

In 1943, a German engineer named Cönders, who worked for Röchling Eisen- und Stahlwerke (which was not just a producer of iron and steel, but had also been active in the field of munitions) proposed an identical weapon. Thanks to the success of one of Cönders' other projects, the so-called 'Röchling Shell' (a bunker-buster par excellence), those who had the all-important ear of the Führer, particularly Albert Speer, the Minister of Munitions, took note. Even though he would only proceed on the understanding that no one, not even the HWA, 'interfered' with his work, Cönders was told to produce a prototype of the *Hochdruckpumpe* ('High-pressure Pump'). He made one in 20mm calibre and obtained satisfactory results, and at that point, Hitler, who had been following progress with interest, decided to take a hand. Cönders would, he decided, build not just one or two guns, but a battery of 50, which would be located in a suitable position behind Calais, aligned towards London some 160km (100 miles) away. A suitable site for what was already being referred to as V3 was found at Marquise-Mimoyecques behind Cap Gris Nez, very close to the southern end of the modern-day Channel Tunnel. This cannot have been altogether easy, when we consider that the V1 and V2 launch sites were already under construction in that same area. There must have been, to say the least, a lively discussion as to which weapon got which piece of real estate. Despite this, work began on two excavations, each of which was to hold an array of 25 guns in 15cm calibre, which would fire long, dart-like projectiles fitted with stabilising fins, which Cönders was even then perfecting. Or, more accurately, which Cönders was not perfecting.

THE HWA TAKES CONTROL

Cönders had built a full-calibre gun at the Hillersleben proving ground, near Magdeburg, and by late 1943 had run into severe problems, both in putting the principle into practice and in producing a workable design for the shell. And even when everything went according to plan – which was seldom – the results were not promising, for muzzle velocity, at just over 1000m (3280ft) per second, was nowhere near high enough. Nonetheless, plans to build a single full-size gun with a barrel 150m (492ft) long at Misdroy near Peenemünde went ahead, while preparation of the site in the Pas de Calais (now reduced to just one following a series of successful bombing raids by the RAF and the USAAF, which had by this time started to pay very close attention to any large engineering work in the area) had reached an advanced stage, and a special artillery battalion was being formed. Still working in isolation, there was little Cönders could do but press on and hope for the best. By mid-March, with no good news coming out of Misdroy, the HWA had had quite enough of this unconventional working arrangement. Senior staff travelled to Misdroy for a demonstration and were less than pleased with what they saw. Generals von Leeb and Schneider of the HWA took control. Matters took a distinct turn for the better as a result. Cönders became but one of the engi-

neers working on the three main problems: projectile design, obturation, and ignition of the subsidiary charges. In all, six different specialist firms including Skoda and Krupp produced satisfactory designs for shells. Obturation problems were solved by placing a sealing piston between the projectile and the initial charge, and that in itself solved the problems of precisely controlling the serial detonation of the subsidiary charges, for now the flash from the original charge couldn't get ahead of the projectile and there was no need to attempt to develop an electrical firing sequence.

By late May, the Misdroy gun was producing more satisfactory results, and ranges of up to about 80km (50 miles) were being reached, when it burst on firing, destroying two sections. New parts were ordered, and a further trial set for early July, but meanwhile the RAF was still at work. After the western site at Marquise had been abandoned, the Todt Organisation, responsible for construction, took great pains to hide the accesses to the eastern site, and for some time it succeeded. However, by late June, the photographic interpreters had decided that there was enough evidence to suggest that something was going on in the area to justify sending Bomber Command's elite 617 Squadron to pay it a visit with 12,000lb (5443kg) 'Tallboy' deep-penetration 'earthquake' bombs. The effect of the raid on 6 July was devastating: one bomb hit the target square-on, and four more scored very near misses which were actually reckoned to be even more effective. The site was put out of commission and no further work was undertaken before it was overrun by Allied troops.

Meanwhile, on 4 July the trials gun had been fired again. This time it got off eight rounds – one of which reached a range of 93km (58 miles) – before it burst, and that effectively put an end to the project to bombard London. There is evidence that further development took place. When Allied troops captured Hillersleben, they found two guns in damaged condition, one with 10 pairs of subsidiary chambers (set at right-angles to the axis of the bore), and the other with five pairs set at a 45-degree angle. Both were 75m (246ft) long. There are unsubstantiated reports that two short-barrelled versions were built and used in combat against US forces during the Battle of the Bulge in December 1944, but experts discount them.

Right: The so-called 'High Pressure Pump' – an innovative approach to the solution of applying greater propulsive force to a projectile. It was never effective.

Tanks and Anti-Tank Weapons

While the British pioneered the use of armoured fighting vehicles in 1916, by 1939 the baton had passed to Germany, where men such as Guderian showed that they could win a war of movement, as British theorists had always promised. Then Hitler took a personal hand in the German tank programme, and his insistence that size mattered above all things was to send the entire effort off on a wild goose chase from which it never fully recovered, even though saner counsel did eventually prevail.

Properly speaking, the tank ceased to be a secret weapon on the morning of 15 September 1916, when the British Tank Mark 1, or 'Mother', went into action on the Somme battlefield. Its appearance came as a complete surprise to the German infantry, secrecy having been maintained throughout. Even the

Above: The Panzerjäger Tiger was based on the vehicle Ferdinand Porsche put forward for the Tiger project.

Left: The 'Panzerschreck' fired a rocket-propelled grenade with a hollow-charge warhead.

name 'tank' was deliberately misleading, though it stuck. More of a secret than the existence of tanks in the German Army was the way in which they would be employed. In any event, their use came as a complete surprise to the Poles in 1939 and to the French the following year. However, that was not to say that new models would be developed in full view.

THE TIGER TANK

When the 58-tonne (57-ton) Sonderkraftfahrzeug (SdKfz) 181 Panzerkampfwagen VI Tiger first went into action on the Leningrad front, 26 years and 1 day

PzKpfw VI TIGER Ausf E
Length (overall): 8.24m (27.00ft)
Width: 3.73m (12.25ft)

Weight: 58,000kg (127,867lb)
Max road speed: 38km/h (24mph)
Max road range: 100km (60 miles)
Crew: 5
Armament: 8.8cm KwK 36 gun;
2 x 7.92mm MG 34 machine guns

after the armoured fighting vehicle made its original debut, it was something the like of which had never been seen. With frontal armour 100mm (3.93in) thick, it was unstoppable at anything but suicidally short range, and its 8.8cm/L56 gun could, quite literally, shoot straight through any vehicle it might happen to meet, the Soviet T-34 which it was specially built to combat being no exception.

In fact, the Tiger's first outing was indecisive, and its second, a week later, much less than successful when one of them bogged down in no-man's-land and had to be blown up to prevent it from falling into enemy hands. It was January of the following year before Tigers went into battle again, and it soon became clear that they were not the omnipotent force they had been thought to be, even though at best, and in the best hands, they were very effective indeed. In the long run, the Tiger would prove to be deeply flawed: its fuel consumption was shocking, and its powerplant and transmission insufficiently robust. By 1944, the Allies had weapons capable of dealing with it, but it seems to have had a place second to none in Adolf Hitler's affections. Certainly it fulfilled all his 'biggest … strongest … best' requirements, at least in the short term. It was eventually to be superseded by the 71.1-tonne (70-ton) SdKfz 182 Tiger II, which was more of everything, and which, despite being even less effective in all but very narrowly defined circumstances, still did not prove to the Führer that the law of diminishing returns was at work.

THE GIANT MOUSE

Hitler is usually held responsible for the decision to build the monster tanks, and he certainly gave them his very active personal approval, but he had a willing

Above: The Tiger was the first of the German 'supertanks', and was effective if properly handled. Its underpowered engine was the cause of many breakdowns, though.

assistant in the person of one Dr Ing. Ferdinand Porsche, who, conveniently, was both the country's leading tank designer (at least, in his own eyes) and head of the Tank Commission. As early as 1942, even before the Tigers had gone into action, Porsche brought forward a plan for a tank he called, presumably with studied irony, the 'Maus' ('Mouse'). This was to be a 152.4-tonne (150-ton) vehicle, with frontal armour a massive 350mm (13.75in) thick, and mounting either a 12.8cm or a 15cm gun with a 7.5cm gun mounted co-axially (as well as a 2cm cannon and two 7.92mm machine guns). Like Porsche's proposed design for the Tiger (which became the Panzerjäger Tiger), the 'Maus' was to have petrol/electric drive, its 1200bhp engine driving a generator, which in turn drove electric motors in the hubs of the driving wheels. This was an elegant enough solution to the many problems of power transmission, but one which would ultimately prove to be flawed, at least on this smaller scale. Submarines and even battleships used it successfully, but in tanks, the motors were not powerful enough and drivers often burned them out trying to extricate their vehicles from difficult situations.

Orders were placed for six prototypes, the first of which was mobile under its own power in December 1943. It proved surprisingly successful, attaining a speed of 20km/h (12.5mph) with an under-spec 1000bhp engine; particularly successful was its suspension system, which was a modified version of Porsche's Tiger's, with longitudinal torsion bars and four interleaved roadwheels per stub-axle. At a total

PzKpfw VI TIGER II Ausf B
Length (overall): 10.26m (33.66ft)
Width: 3.75m (12.29ft)

Weight: 71,100kg (156,747lb)
Max road speed: 38km/h (24mph)
Max road range: 110km
(68 miles)
Crew: 5
Armament: 8.8cm KwK 43 gun;
2 x 7.92mm MG 34 machine guns

weight of almost 193 tonnes (190 tons) including its six-man crew, fuel and ordnance, there was hardly a road bridge in the country which would have taken its weight, and thus it was designed from the outset to be able to submerge to a depth of 8m (26.25ft), air for occupants and powerplant being supplied via a schnorkel tube which extended from the turret roof. The 'Maus' project didn't get much further than the initial stage; in all, nine prototypes had been wholly or partially completed by the war's end, though that

Below: A pair of knocked-out Tigers in the Soviet Union in 1944. By that time the Allies had got the measure of these 58-tonne (57-ton) monsters.

Above: The King Tiger was heavier than the Tiger and had a more powerful 8.8cm gun. It was, however, also prone to breakdowns, having the same powerplant as the Tiger.

small result does not reflect the amount of energy, money and scarce resources which had been lavished on it. And worse was to come, because the HWA – having protested that it did not want such a vehicle and could formulate no sensible tactical plan for its use, and having been overruled by the Führer – then decided to commission something very similar itself!

It comes as no surprise to find that it was to Henschel, the producer of both versions of the Tiger (and of the much more successful PzKpfw V Panther), that

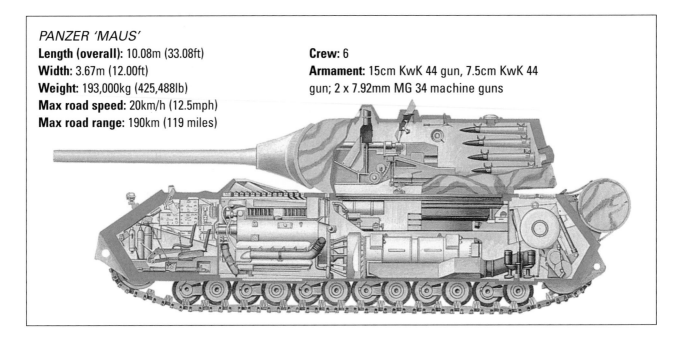

PANZER 'MAUS'
Length (overall): 10.08m (33.08ft)
Width: 3.67m (12.00ft)
Weight: 193,000kg (425,488lb)
Max road speed: 20km/h (12.5mph)
Max road range: 190km (119 miles)

Crew: 6
Armament: 15cm KwK 44 gun, 7.5cm KwK 44 gun; 2 x 7.92mm MG 34 machine guns

the HWA turned, and even less of one to learn that the E100, as the project was known, displayed more than a passing resemblance to them, though it was certainly on a grander scale. Its all-up weight was estimated at 142.2 tonnes (140 tons) which would probably have meant it going into battle at least 10.16 tonnes (10 tons) heavier, and it, too, was to have had the KwK 44 15cm gun and a co-axially mounted 7.5cm. In all, it appears to have been a more realistic (though the phrase is used loosely) proposition than the Maus. One prototype was under construction at the war's end, but had never run.

In all, the German tank development programme during World War II was deeply flawed by the assumption that a single vehicle, heavily armoured and with a powerful gun, would be able to out-fight (or at least out-range) any number of enemy tanks. By the time the Allies landed in Normandy in 1944, this was certainly not true. American Sherman tanks, which appeared on the battlefield around the same time as the Tiger, had by then acquired very much more powerful guns – the 76mm in American-manned tanks, the 17pdr in British service – and had a fighting chance which their numerical superiority turned into a certainty. The same was true in the east with the up-gunned T-34. It would have been very much more sensible to have abandoned the Tiger (or better still, never to have begun it) and to have concentrated instead on the PzKpfw V Panther, which many experts rate as the best tank of the entire war. Certainly, Panthers were quicker (and much cheaper) to produce, and were formidable opponents, with a

Above: Even the King Tiger would have been dwarfed beside the 'Maus'. Its secondary armament was to have been the 7.5cm gun, the Panther tank's main armament.

KwK 42 7.5cm cannon, 70 calibres long, developed by Rheinmetall-Borsig, which was capable of perforating any Allied tank at virtually all ranges.

ANTI-TANK WEAPONS

If the German tank development programme was fatally flawed, the same could not be said of the anti-tank (AT) weapons development programme. At the start of World War II, anti-tank weapons were simply not up to the task, save in a few particulars. One was the heavy German 8.8cm gun, which had started life as an anti-aircraft weapon but which showed itself during the Spanish Civil War as a very successful AT weapon, once appropriate armour-piercing projectiles had been developed. It soon acquired a practical and practicable mobile mounting, and was issued as the Panzerabwehrkanone (PaK) 36; it was also adopted as the KwK 36 for the Tiger tank. It was very capable, but entirely conventional; other German developments in high-velocity guns intended for use against armoured vehicles were not.

THE TAPERED-BORE GUNS

The earliest suggestion for a gun with a uniformly tapering barrel seems to have originated in Germany in about 1903 with a man named Karl Puff. He suggested using a projectile with a sleeve, which was compressed by the taper of the bore until it filled a series of grooves in the body of the bullet. By that means, the velocity of the projectile was much increased, since its cross-sectional area had been diminished considerably while the pressure in the barrel remained constant (the velocity being a product of the two). Unfortunately for Puff, the complexities of manufacturing a rifled tapered bore were beyond the capability of German gunmakers, and nothing came of the idea, at least, not then.

In the 1930s, another German, a gunmaker named Hermann Gerlich, experimented with Puff's scheme, and was able to manufacture hunting rifles according to the principle. They proved to be excellent, with the all-important flat trajectory, but when he tried to interest the armed services of a number of countries in such a rifle, he was less successful, entirely, it seems, thanks to the projected cost of the weapon. However, the Springfield Arsenal, for one, certainly validated the concept, producing a version of the M1917 rifle with a muzzle velocity of over 2135m/s (7000ft/s) instead of the standard 855m/s (2800ft/s). Gerlich gave up trying to market the concept himself in 1933, and contacted Rheinmetall, who saw the possibility of incorporating the system into an anti-tank rifle, using a projectile with a tungsten carbide core and soft steel skirt. Eventually, it produced what became known as the Panzerbüchse (anti-tank rifle) 41, which fired a 20mm (it had started out at 28mm nominal diameter) round at a muzzle velocity of around 1400m/s (4600ft/s), and which could perforate (ie, pass completely through) 66mm (2.6in) of nickel-steel armour at a range of 500m (1640ft). Soon, Rheinmetall produced a more powerful version in 4.2cm nominal calibre, which squeezed its projectiles down to 29.4mm, and which could perforate that same thickness of armour plate at twice the distance. It entered service in 1941 as the 4.2cm Panzerabwehrkanone (anti-tank gun) 41, and proved to be very successful.

THE SQUEEZE-BORE GUN

Two years earlier, Krupp had also begun to examine the possibilities of reducing the cross-sectional area of a projectile while it was in the barrel, and settled on a slightly simpler, but no less effective, method of carrying out the procedure. Instead of manufacturing a barrel with a uniformly tapered bore, Krupp added a smooth-bore, step-tapered section to the muzzle of a conventional gun. The (flanged) round entered the supplementary section at nominal diameter of 7.5cm and passed through two tapered sections which reduced it to 5.5cm. The advantage of this was chiefly

Above: The 8.8cm Raketenwerfer 43, usually called the 'Püppchen', was not a gun but a rocket launcher. It was superseded by the shoulder-held tube rocket launchers.

logistical; only the unrifled, tapered section became badly worn (that, of course, was the system's great drawback), and was attached to the main section of the barrel by a simple screw collar, which meant it could be replaced in the field without the need for special tools. The 7.5cm PaK 41, as the gun was known, fired a tungsten-cored shot weighing 2.6kg (5.7lb) at a muzzle velocity of 1125m/s (3700ft/s) and could perforate 125mm (4.9in) of armour, more than any tank had, at a range of 2000m (6560ft). This gun was the weapon originally specified for the Tiger tank. The taper-bore and squeeze-bore guns were without question excellent battlefield weapons, but they needed tungsten for their bullet cores if they were to be effective, and that was a material in short supply in Germany at that time, being much in demand in the engineering industry as cutter bits for machine tools. Eventually, a choice had to be made, and the manufacturing industry won. The taper-bore and squeeze-bore guns were taken out of service and scrapped and few survived the war. Rheinmetall and Krupp offered conventional anti-tank guns in larger calibres instead, culminating in the 12.8cm PaK 44.

SHAPED AND HOLLOW CHARGES

The kinetic energy of a very hard object travelling at high speed (brute force, in other words) was one way to perforate armour, but there was another: the shaped

Above: The Panzerfaust 30 was the simplest of all German rocket-propelled grenade launchers. Its designation referred to its optimum range – 30m (32.8 yards).

Below: Appearances are not deceptive. The 'Panzerschreck' was developed from the US Bazooka, and was just as effective. Two versions were produced.

or hollow explosive charge, which incorporated a hollow cone or hemisphere of metal translated by the heat of the explosion behind it into a high-speed (around 7500m/s; 24,600ft/s) jet of molten material and gas. This was first produced, in Germany in 1939, as a demolition charge, and is reputed to have been first used in combat at the storming of the fortress of Eben-Emael in May 1940. By that time, however, its developers had moved on, and were on the verge of producing an artillery shell on the same principle.

The British and Americans had also made considerable progress independently, while the Soviets had achieved the same ends by the rather simpler means of copying captured or stolen German munitions. However, in this principle, there was a problem: the act of spinning the shell to maintain its accuracy in flight dispersed the molten jet and made it much less effective. One answer was to stabilise the round with fins instead, but that took some working out. Another answer was to emulate the pyrotechnic 'sky rocket' and fit the projectile with a long shaft for a tail. In the successful German development of this simple principle, the rod was surrounded by a tube upon which fins were mounted. The rod went down the barrel of a 3.7cm PaK 36 anti-tank gun, and the tube fitted around it, with the shaped-charge warhead, with its copper hemisphere and 2.4kg (5.3lb) of TNT and hexogen sitting in front of the muzzle. It was propelled by

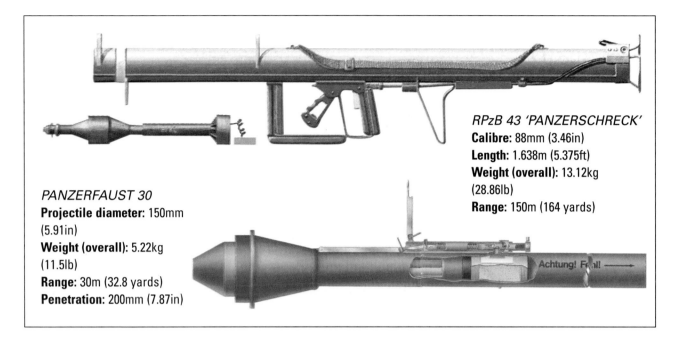

RPzB 43 'PANZERSCHRECK'
Calibre: 88mm (3.46in)
Length: 1.638m (5.375ft)
Weight (overall): 13.12kg (28.86lb)
Range: 150m (164 yards)

PANZERFAUST 30
Projectile diameter: 150mm (5.91in)
Weight (overall): 5.22kg (11.5lb)
Range: 30m (32.8 yards)
Penetration: 200mm (7.87in)

a special cartridge, loaded conventionally at the breech, and was reasonably accurate up to about 300m (985ft). Being independent of the kinetic energy of the round in flight (which diminished with distance, of course) the warhead was equally effective at all ranges, and could pierce 180mm (7.08in) of armour. The shaped-charge warhead was also to be mated with simple solid-fuel rocket 'motors' to produce early RPGs (rocket-propelled grenades), the Panzerfaust and the Raketenpanzerbüchse (also known as the 'Panzerschreck' – 'panzer terror'), which was a direct copy of the American Rocket Launcher M1, the celebrated Bazooka, using German 8.8cm rockets.

THE RUHRSTAHL X-7 'ROTTKÄPPCHEN'

An altogether more elegant solution to the problem of killing tanks on the battlefield at something greater than suicidally close quarters (the main problem with the Panzerfaust and 'Panzerschreck') was put forward by Ruhrstahl. We have already encountered this company as the producers of the 'Fritz-X' guided bomb and the X-4 air-to-air guided missile, in response to HWA's request in 1944. The X-7 'Rottkäppchen' ('Red Riding Hood') was essentially similar in nature to the X-4 AAM, with its conventional HE warhead exchanged for a 2.5kg (5.5lb) shaped charge, and with its control system cunningly simplified. Like the X-4, the X-7 was winged (two wings only, in this case, with parabolic leading and trailing edges, with spools from which the control wire paid out located at their tips) and revolved slowly in flight, both pitch and yaw

Above: The Raketenpanzerbüchse 43 'Panzerschreck' and the simpler Panzerfaust gave even individual infantrymen the means to kill tanks.

being controlled by a single spade-like vane or fin mounted at the end of a curved arm which, when the missile was launched, hung down and behind the body. As the missile rotated (once again, at a rate of about one complete turn per second), this was able to exercise control over both pitch and yaw, a gyroscopic switch transferring the signals to actuate the simple spoiler as it turned from the vertical to the horizontal plane and so on, an elegant solution indeed.

The X-7 was powered by two WASAG solid-fuel rockets whose diglycol propellant was in the form of two concentric tubes. The first charge gave a thrust of 68kg (150lb) for two and a half seconds to launch the missile into flight and get it up to its 360km/h (224 mph) operating speed; the second gave 5.5kg (12lb) of thrust for eight seconds (which was actually longer by a considerable margin than the flight was likely to last) to sustain it. Maximum range was to have been around 1200m (1310 yards). It is thought that a total of a few hundred Ruhrstahl X-7s were manufactured, and that most were consumed in testing, but there is some evidence to suggest that some made it into the field, and were expended in combat on the Eastern Front during 1945. There are unconfirmed reports that the X-7 performed satisfactorily, and was able to deal even with the JS-1 'Stalin' heavy tank, which was impervious to virtually everything else at anything over short range.

CHAPTER ELEVEN

Submarines and their Weapons

By the time World War II was halfway through, Germany (and in particular the Führer himself) had largely given up on its surface navy, but the submarine arm was another matter entirely. U-boat veterans knew, however, that much still remained to be developed in the boats themselves, and a well-funded programme was put into effect. Yet again it proved to be just too late, however, for by the time the new-generation boats were coming off the ways, the war was already lost.

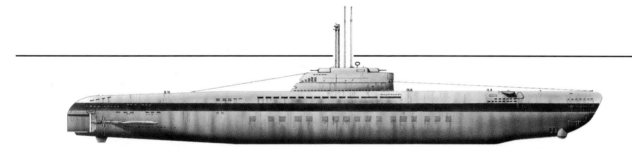

If the Luftwaffe was the Nazi Party favourite in pre-war and wartime Germany, the *Kriegsmarine* (Navy) was, for a variety of reasons, very definitely not. Some of the reasons were historical and political, and went back to the dark days of near civil war in the 1920s, but others were more recently rooted, and had to do exclusively with the poor performance of German capital ships. At one point, an enraged Hitler actually ordered all the surface fleet to be scrapped. The exception was the submarine service which, under the talented leadership of Karl Dönitz, had

Above: The Type XXI U-boat was one of the most influential naval developments of the twentieth century.

Left: Germany also developed midget submarines, like this 'Biber' putting to sea from Rotterdam at Christmas 1944.

actually come close to cutting Britain's vital lifeline to the United States and to its colonies. Most of the few funds for development that did find their way to the *Kriegsmarine* were destined for the U-boat arm.

HOMING TORPEDOES AND MAGNETIC MINES

By the end of World War I, the submarine torpedo, the first really successful model of which had been produced by the Anglo-Italian Whitehead in 1868, had been developed to the point where it was a reliable, practical weapon. During that war it had been used to sink thousands of ships (German submarines alone accounted for 5556), and we can hazard a guess that the individual success rate (expressed as hits per torpedo) probably made it one of the most effective offensive weapons of the whole conflict. However, it was a relatively simple, unsophisticated weapon, and that, combined with its effectiveness, surely meant that it could be improved. There was certainly the possibility of giving it much greater endurance and straight-line performance, but increasing the range always resulted in a lowering of the strike rate, since the torpedoes had no self-directive capability. There is reason to believe that scientists in Germany had actually perfected a passive acoustic homing device to steer a torpedo towards a submarine sound source by 1936, and that the new weapon had been kept back from production to preserve its secrecy.

FOXING THE 'FOXER'

The relatively simple first-generation devices, which were restricted to fairly low speeds, proved effective against slow-moving targets such as merchant ships, but less so against warships, which often simply outpaced them. Towed noise-makers (known as 'Foxers'; originally no more than two lengths of iron pipe,

Below: *U1406*, one of the few operational Type XVII Walter-engined boats to be completed. She was scuttled in May 1945 but was salvaged and taken to the United States. A sister-boat, *U1407*, went to the UK.

chained loosely together so that they constantly crashed into each other) could also dupe these devices, and it was September 1943 before German scientists perfected a means of outwitting them.

When a torpedo fitted with the second-generation T5 or 'Zaunkönig' ('Wren') passive acoustic seeker detected a sound source in a small arc ahead of it, a subsidiary circuit operated a simple solenoid switch to actuate the small rudder vane. This caused the torpedo to turn sharply to starboard and run in a circular path for a predetermined period (long enough, in fact, for it to describe a semi-circle) before turning sharply to starboard once more and setting off on its original track again. In this way, the torpedo skirted the noise-maker and homed in on the propeller noise of the ship towing it instead. Then, on encountering the noise of the ship dead ahead, the torpedo turned to perform the circling manoeuvre once more. The diameter of the semi-circular track the torpedo described being less than the length of the ship plus the distance the latter covered in the intervening period, it would strike the target from the beam. It has been estimated that 700 T5s were fired in anger, and that 77 (11 per cent) scored hits. The US Navy introduced the similarly

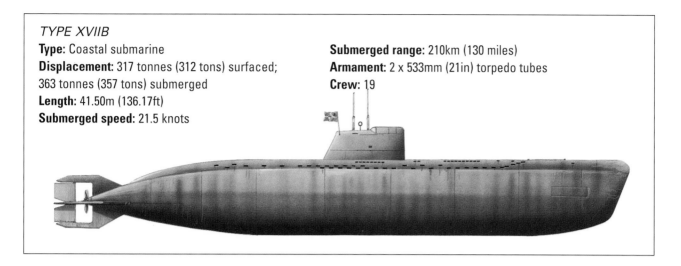

TYPE XVIIB

Type: Coastal submarine
Displacement: 317 tonnes (312 tons) surfaced;
363 tonnes (357 tons) submerged
Length: 41.50m (136.17ft)
Submerged speed: 21.5 knots

Submerged range: 210km (130 miles)
Armament: 2 x 533mm (21in) torpedo tubes
Crew: 19

equipped Mark 27 torpedo in 1944, and in the last years of the war, 106 were fired in combat, scoring 33 hits (31 per cent).

Another approach was to fit a form of automatic pilot, which caused the torpedo to make a series of pre-programmed turns after it had run a preset distance, in the hope that a torpedo fired in the general direction of a convoy would turn and hit a ship purely by chance. Neither the success rate of the Federapparat-Torpedo, nor that of its more sophisticated successor, the Lagenunabhängiger-Torpedo (which could be fired from depths of up to 50m; 164ft), seems to have been recorded. Later U-boats had their six forward-facing torpedo tubes organised into an array which covered 10 degrees of arc; firing all six in a salvo gave a much-improved chance of hitting the target. It is obvious that the same guidance system which was applied to the glider bombs and the guided missiles could also have been applied to torpedoes, even though keeping a precise track of the missile's course would naturally have been more difficult. It is inconceivable that an experimental programme, at least, was not initiated. Certainly, one of the *Kriegsmarine*'s original submarine warfare instructors, Werner Fürbringer, suggested it.

A viable alternative to the torpedo was to lay mines in the path of the oncoming enemy (particularly if this was a slow-moving convoy), and a variety of submarine-launched mines were developed. The Torpedo-Ankertaumine (TMA) had a 215kg (475lb) explosive charge, and was attached to an anchor which allowed it to float at a predetermined height, while the Torpedo-Grundminen lay on the seabed in shallower water. They came in two sizes: the 500kg (1100lb) TMB and the 1000kg (2200lb) TMC. All three mines were dimensioned to allow them to be deployed

Above: The Type XVII boats had both conventional diesel engines and a single Walter closed-cycle engine. They were designed for coastal operations.

through a standard 533mm (21in) torpedo tube and could be fitted with a variety of remotely actuated detonators, magnetic or acoustic.

THE NEW GENERATION OF SUBMARINES

There was little development of the basic submarine in the inter-war period, except that the once-popular saddle-tank design, in which the buoyancy chambers were located outside the pressure hull, gave way more and more to the double hull, in which they enclosed it almost completely and were themselves contained within a light enclosure which could be shaped to improve sea-keeping and performance. In Germany, developments in the late 1930s were aimed only at increasing the size and endurance of existing types, not making any radical changes to their design. However, by 1941, experimental boats with a new type of powerplant which did not need atmospheric oxygen had been produced, and were proving to be quite remarkable. The powerplant in question was, once again, the creation of the prolific Professor Hellmuth Walter, whom we have already met.

Walter had constructed a small experimental boat, the *V80*, launched on 19 January 1940, which displaced just 73.8 tonnes (75 tons) submerged. He equipped it with a steam turbine, fed by a variant of the liquid-fuel motors which were to power the V1 flying bomb's launch catapult, producing their steam by the chemical reaction of hydrogen peroxide with a catalyst. Walter soon discovered that his submarine could make almost 30 knots submerged – around three times the submerged speed of any conventional

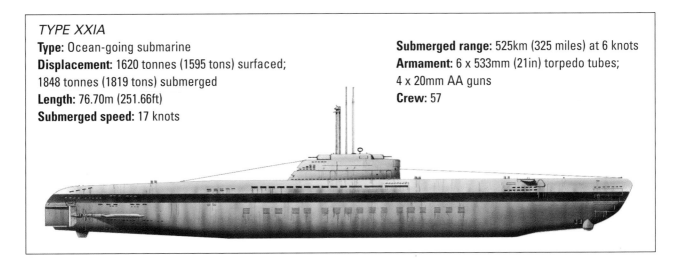

TYPE XXIA
Type: Ocean-going submarine
Displacement: 1620 tonnes (1595 tons) surfaced;
1848 tonnes (1819 tons) submerged
Length: 76.70m (251.66ft)
Submerged speed: 17 knots

Submerged range: 525km (325 miles) at 6 knots
Armament: 6 x 533mm (21in) torpedo tubes;
4 x 20mm AA guns
Crew: 57

Above: The Type XXIs were ocean-going submarines of over 1600 tonnes (1575 tons), the size of a small destroyer of the period. They could make 17 knots submerged.

submarine running on battery power – and that led him to suggest to the *Kriegsmarine* the construction of a fleet of similarly powered submarine warships. When asked where he proposed to store the large quantities of reagent and fuel that would be required, he produced a design for a two-decker submarine, in itself virtually two existing double hulls joined into a figure '8', the bottom portion of which would serve

exclusively as 'bunkerage'. Someone at this proposal meeting noted that it would be just as easy to fill that lower section with batteries.

THE 'ELECTRO-BOATS'

Whatever the method adopted, as the war wore on, it was to become harder and harder for U-boat commanders to remain on the surface, even at night,

Below: The conning tower top of a (scuttled) Type XXI. Note the retractable radio antenna and the faired-in machine gun emplacements.

TYPE XXIII
Type: Coastal submarine
Displacement: 233 tonnes
(230 tons) surfaced; 260 tonnes
(256 tons) submerged
Length: 34.7m (113.75ft)
Submerged speed: 22 knots

Submerged range: 325km
(202 miles) at 4 knots
Armament: 2 x 533mm (21in)
torpedo tubes
Crew: 14

Above: The other 'Electro-boats' were the much smaller Type XXIIIs, intended for coastal operations. Even with a complement of just 14, they were cramped, much of the interior being given over to batteries.

thanks to the increasingly effective airborne anti-submarine patrols mounted by the RAF and the USAAF. If they were to continue to wage war effectively, they would have to be provided with boats which could stay submerged for extended periods and perform more effectively under water, and it was along these lines that the bulk of research was carried out. More 'Walter' boats were built or at least were in the course of construction when the war ended. The two Type XVIIB boats which were successfully salvaged after having been scuttled in Hamburg harbour were later transferred to the US Navy and the Royal Navy, who operated them experimentally, but the powerplant required massive quantities of fairly exotic fuel and was most temperamental. It would perhaps become a valid solution in the fullness of time, but that was something the *Kriegsmarine* did not have, and it was essential to look at other suggestions.

THE TYPE XXI AND TYPE XXIII

The off-the-cuff remark to Walter about using the lower-deck space of his two-deck submarine for batteries was to have far-reaching consequences, and to lead to the construction of two classes of submarines which were actually faster submerged than they were on the surface: the ocean-going Type XXI; and the smaller, coastal Type XXIII. They were not the first to so perform; right at the end of World War I, the British constructed a class of 'hunter-killer' submarines, the 'R' class, with the 220-volt batteries taken from the much bigger 'J' class, combined with a spindle-form

hull from an earlier era, with a speed on the surface of 9.5 knots and 15 knots submerged. They proved to be difficult to control, and were stricken prematurely, though *R4* stayed in service until the early 1930s.

The two types of German combat submarines were quite different in character. The Type XXIII was strictly for local deployment in coastal waters, if only by virtue of its size. It displaced 233 tonnes (230 tons) on the surface, was 34.7m (113.8ft) long and 3m (9.8ft) abeam, and had a crew of just 14. Its biggest weakness as a warship was that it carried just two 533mm (21in) torpedoes, pre-loaded into two bow tubes, and no re-loads. Almost 500 were scheduled to be built at yards in Germany (Kiel and Hamburg), France (Toulon), Italy (Genoa and Montefalcone), and Russia (Nikolaev), but only the German yards of Deutsche Werft and Germaniawerft actually launched any boats, the German Army having been driven back out of occupied territory before any could be completed. The first boat, *U2321*, was launched at Hamburg on 17 April 1944 and a total of 63 had been completed by the time the war ended. However, problems of commissioning meant that only 10 operational patrols were made from March to May 1945; six merchant ships were sunk, two of them, by *U2336*, off Scotland on 7 May, being amongst the last sinkings of the war.

As its powerplant, the Type XXIII had a single 580bhp MWM diesel engine which drove two electric motors either directly or via the extensive batteries. The principal electric motor produced 580shp and could produce a submerged top speed of 22 knots; the secondary, 'creeping', motor produced just 35shp for a speed of 5 knots, but in almost complete silence. Using the secondary motor alone, the submarine could stay submerged, making a speed of 4 knots, for

40 hours. Like the bigger, Type XXI boats, they were streamlined in appearance, with all external fittings either faired-in or removed.

The Type XXI was a more sophisticated boat than the Type XXIII; it was 76.7m (251.6ft) long and 6.6m (21.6ft) abeam, displacing 1620 tonnes (1595 tons) on the surface. Type XXIs were equipped with six torpedo tubes, all of them situated in the bow, and a total of 23 torpedoes (they were also to have carried four 30mm anti-aircraft cannon, but never did, a pair of 20mm cannon being substituted). Like the coastal boats, they were double-decked, the frames being fitted outside the pressure hulls, which suited the modular, prefabricated building method by then in use in Germany. Their powerplants were considerably more powerful, of course: they had two MAN diesels of 1000bhp each driving two propeller shafts via two 1250shp electric motors or two 57shp 'creeping' motors; on the surface they could make 15.5 knots and submerged, on main engines, over 17 knots, with 5 knots available from the auxiliary motors.

Almost 700 Type XXIs were scheduled to have been built by Blohm & Voss in Hamburg, Deschimag in Bremen, and Schichau in Danzig (Gdansk), but only 121 were actually commissioned. Many more were bombed on the slip prior to launching and a substantial number remained incomplete at the end of the war. Some of them – and some of the boats already in commission – were taken to the Soviet Union and completed there and formed the backbone of the Red Navy's submarine arm for many years. Indeed, so greedy were the Soviets for German submarines that they loaded the hangar decks of the incomplete hull of the aircraft carrier *Graf Zeppelin* with U-boat hull sections and proceeded to tow it the length of the Baltic to Leningrad, but it hit a mine in the Gulf of Finland and sank. Only two Type XXI boats ever left port on operational patrols and neither fired a shot in anger. The advance in submarine operations which the Type XXI and Type XXIII represented cannot be overstated. They altered the world's navies' perceptions of what could be expected of a submarine, and every design later produced, up to the modern 'teardrops', reflected that.

Left: The head of an extensible induction mast, or schnorkel tube. It took considerable ingenuity to produce a self-regulating valve system which was fast-enough acting to prevent large quantities of water being sucked into the submarine. The Dutch were the first to find a solution to the problem in about 1936.

Above: A 'Marder' ('Marten') midget submarine being launched by crane. The nature of the craft – it was no more than a torpedo with a small crew compartment replacing the warhead – is obvious.

Below: The 'Molch' ('Salamander') was slightly more sophisticated than the 'Marder'. It carried two underslung torpedoes and around 400 were built. The 'Molch' was used against Allied shipping in the Scheldt.

THE SCHNORKEL

There was one more way to keep the boat submerged with its engines running, of course: let it breathe through a tube. This may seem an obvious solution, and indeed, the very earliest submariners had adopted it, but in a large boat travelling even at only 5 or so knots, a breathing tube was very difficult indeed to maintain in operation in anything but a flat-calm sea. The practical problems were largely solved, however, by about 1936, and in a somewhat unlikely quarter: the Netherlands. When the German Army invaded in May 1940, examples of submarines with functional extensible induction masts (as the breathing tubes are properly known) were captured intact, but were never copied, and those fitted to Dutch submarines which the *Kriegsmarine* put into operation were removed. German submarine commanders' policy was to remain on the surface as much as possible, and only submerge to avoid escape or to make a particularly risky attack. As a result, U-boat commanders had no use for the snorting mast, at least, not until the dark days of 1943, when they were regularly being forced to dive by anti-submarine patrols, and when a research programme was put in hand to replicate the

results the Dutch had achieved. The first German submarine to have been fitted with a schnorkel seems to have been *U264*, and she was lost in February 1944 during her initial attempt to use it. Some experts maintain that the first-generation schnorkels caused as many problems as they solved, but they achieved their major objective of allowing the submarine to run submerged on its diesel engines, even if was a tricky business, and unpopular with the crew, who had been accustomed to a short watch on deck every now and then. It could also be very dangerous, as the loss of *U264* indicates, as it was all too easy to run the head-valve (a simple ball valve at the end of the U-shaped top section of the induction tube) under water, whereupon the diesels would begin to suck the air out of the boat's interior and would create a very considerable under-pressure before they stopped.

MIDGET SUBMARINES

Given their almost complete lack of success, it comes as something of a surprise to discover the extent of the German Navy's midget submarine programme. At least six different types of craft were produced in considerable numbers – certainly over 1500 in total – from 1943 (the programme was behind those of Britain, Italy, and especially Japan). The first types would more accurately be called semi-submersibles, for they all ran with their upper surfaces barely awash, the solitary crewman being able to see out through ports in the vestigial conning tower which enclosed his head. The first constructed was known as the 'Hecht' ('Pike'); it was battery-powered and really little more than a manned torpedo with a detachable warhead. An improved model, the 'Neger' ('Negro') had a petrol engine, and carried an underslung torpedo. It worked well enough, but its solitary crewman had to breathe oxygen, and was thus restricted in what he could do. Two larger one-man types, the 'Molch' ('Salamander') and the 'Marder' ('Marten'), were slightly more practical, with recirculating air supplies. The former carried two underslung torpedoes, and was used with some success against Allied shipping in the Scheldt in late 1944 and 1945. The 'Marder' carried just one torpedo but could submerge completely in order to attack.

Below: The 'Biber' ('Beaver') was the third one-man midget submarine type. It could be transported by road or by specially equipped 'mother' submarines and proved to be quite successful in 1944–45.

Above: The best of all the German World War II midget submarines was the two-man 15.2-tonne (15-ton) 'Seehund' ('Seal'), the only type which was truly capable of operating independently.

The next step was to produce a true submersible, a proper submarine in miniature. The first attempt resulted in a single-seater experimental vehicle called the 'Hai' ('Shark'), powered by a petrol engine and batteries, which could make 20 knots for two hours on its electric motor. The 'Hai' was developed into the one-man 'Biber' ('Beaver'), which displaced 3.04 tonnes (3 tons) and carried two torpedoes slung beneath the hull; a later version of the 'Biber' was capable of carrying a second crewmember. Over 300 were built and used with a measure of success in the Scheldt Estuary and off Murmansk in the convoy assembly area. The 'Biber' could be transported by road or by air as well as by specially modified conventional submarines.

The most successful of the German midget submarines was the two-man 'Seehund' ('Seal'). This was much bigger at 15.2 tonnes (15 tons) displacement, and had jettisonable auxiliary fuel tanks, which gave it a range of around 800km (500 miles). It could make 8 knots on the surface and 6 knots submerged. The 'Seehund' also gained some success in the mouth of the Scheldt. Unconfirmed reports from German sources claim that it also operated against merchant shipping in the Thames estuary and off Margate.

CHAPTER TWELVE

Nuclear, Biological and Chemical Weapons

When war broke out in 1939, it was feared that poison gas would be used even more widely than it had been in World War I. To that fear was added the threat of biological agents, while physicists were struggling with the possibility of harnessing nuclear fission to produce a bomb the likes of which had never been seen.

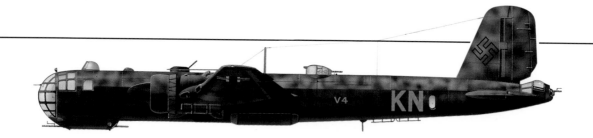

In December 1938, German physicists Otto Hahn and Fritz Strassman demonstrated the fission (splitting) of the uranium atom. This caused a stir in the scientific community, and ripples spread outside it, even as far as the HWA, to which several scientists wrote, suggesting that the phenomenon might conceivably be used in a bomb. The notion made slow progress, but by late 1939 a steering committee had

Above: The Heinkel He 177A-5; an He 177 was modified to carry the never-completed German atom bomb.

Left: A US serviceman is confronted by massed ranks of German mustard gas shells after the war.

been formed. It had just one item on its agenda: could a nuclear reactor to produce fissionable material be built? As a rider, subsidiary questions were posed about costs and timescale. A research programme was drawn up, and six university-based projects were established. By 1941, it had become clear that the notion was feasible, and the steering committee reported to HWA that a reactor could and should be built, and that it should use as its moderator, deutrium, also known as 'heavy water'. The entire project went downhill from there, but it would be a long while before that was to become obvious. By 1942, five different laboratories were experimenting with atomic piles, each one with a different theory of how it should be constructed, and each one in ignorance of what the others were (or were not) doing. At least one team – that led by Werner Heisenberg, Nobel laureate and dean of the German physics community, who had recently been appointed Director of the Kaiser Wilhelm Institute at Dahlem – is reported to have deliberately exploited the confusion which resulted to drag its feet. Convinced that a bomb could be contructed, Heisenberg set out to slow the process down, and make as little actual progress as possible towards its conclusion. Eventually, Albert Speer, Hitler's Minister for Munitions, lost patience, and demanded from Heisenberg a prediction of the length of time which would be required to actually manufacture a bomb. Heisenberg prevaricated still, but eventually said that he believed it might be possible by 1945.

Speer decided to set up a single research project charged with constructing a reactor. He assembled some of the best brains in the field and asked them to submit a budget. They requested 40,000 Reichsmarks, less than the cost of a single PzKpfw IV tank, and this, more than anything, seems to have convinced him that the project had a very low likelihood of success. From then on, it seems, the nuclear research programme concentrated on producing a reactor suitable for power generation, rather than one to produce fissionable material for a bomb. Naturally, such a power station would inevitably produce small quantities of fissionable material as a by-product, but it would be a very long time before it would be possible to build a bomb, even if the reactor worked perfectly.

Two atomic piles were eventually built, one near Hechingen, the other near Erfurt, both using deutrium as their moderator. Neither actually achieved a chain reaction, largely because they were too small. By that time – late 1944 – the infrastructure of German industry was becoming increasingly chaotic. Such small supplies of uranium ore as were available – from a small field in Belgium and another in Bohemia – were running low, and thanks to a successful bombing raid by the RAF on the deutrium production plant in Norway, that was in short supply too. The programme was already dead in its infancy, and one might even say that it was stillborn.

There was perhaps a subsidiary use of uranium as a weapon of war under consideration. In 1943, HWA commissioned a report from a biological laboratory on the toxicity of radioactive material. From this it has been widely concluded that uranium dust was to have been employed as cargo in a conventional high-explosive bomb or rocket warhead, but there is no firm evidence to support this speculation and certainly no evidence to suggest that even the most basic experimentation ever took place outside the laboratory. One could just as well conclude that the project was aimed at improving worker safety.

BIOLOGICAL WEAPONS

Outside very special limits, suicidal attacks make little tactical sense, and a suicidal strategy makes none at all. Those truisms have always done more than pure ethics or morality to control the use of one of the most dreadful potential weapons known to man: disease. Indeed, in limited 'experiments', where the vectors of the disease in question could be completely controlled, man has shown himself willing to use biological agents of death. The US Army used it in the form of smallpox-infected blankets distributed to native Americans, and the Japanese did too in Manchuria in the 1930s. But as an everyday weapon of war, it had one enormous disadvantage: it was as likely to kill you, in the long run, as it was to kill your enemy. That is not to say that every country did not have its biological warfare research establishments, but more to suggest that much of the research carried out in them was aimed more at providing a defence against the agents of disease. There are persistent reports that tests of biological agents were carried out on unwill-

Left: Like all armies, the Wehrmacht took chemical weapons very seriously, as the protective clothing and warning signs on this locker indicate.

ing participants in concentration and extermination camps in Germany, and in the light of other undeniable findings from the people investigating the events in those places, we have to leave the question open.

CHEMICAL WEAPONS

More than half a century on, there is no lessening of the revulsion felt against the obscenities committed in the Nazi death camps or against the men and women who actually committed the acts, and that is as it should be. But besides the ethical and moral aspects, there is also the purely practical to be considered, for the destruction of six million or more people could only proceed on an industrial scale. The mass murders had to carried out under factory conditions. Very soon it became obvious that the only acceptable method would be by mass poisoning, the toxin to be delivered in the form of a gas. In the event, this murder of millions of helpless people was to be the only widespread use of chemical warfare during World War II. This is apart from Italian forces using phosgene in Abyssinia in 1938, the Japanese use of it in China from the mid-1930s to the end of 1941 in some 840 separate incidents, and reports that something described as 'toxic smoke' was used during the siege of Sebastopol.

German troops initiated the use of gas as a weapon of war in February 1915, when they fired shells filled with xylyl bromide (a lachrymogen, or tear gas) against Russian forces. The operation failed, for the gas was frozen solid in the shells, and dispersed only very slowly. Two months later, they used chlorine gas against British and Empire troops at Ypres with greater success, and from then on it became a recognised part of both sides' armouries. But it was not that effective; gas was responsible for only just over one per cent of battlefield deaths during the entire war. It was slightly more effective as a wounding agent – 5.69 per cent of all injuries were caused by gas – and from a military point of view, wounding is actually more desirable, since caring for wounded both on and off the battlefield eats into precious resources.

By 1919, there was a limited repertoire of gases available: chlorine, mustard gas, phosgene and a few others. By the time two decades had passed, there was a whole menu of more effective agents available, including some very exotic compounds which had been produced during research into insecticides and herbicides. These compounds were organo-phosphates, and were to become the basis for what we now call nerve gases. The original nerve gas, known as Tabun, was first synthesised in 1936 into a substance

Above: The sinister facade of a German mustard gas storage building, in which the agent was kept in huge concrete vats.

called ethyl-dimethyl-amido-phosphor-cyanidate. By 1942, a factory to produce it to the tune of 1016 tonnes (1000 tons) per month had been established at Dyhernfurth in Silesia (now Brzeg Dolny in Poland). In 1938, a second and even more effective organo-phosphate, isopropyl methyl-phosphoro-fluoridate, was synthesised. Known as Sarin, it proved to be very much harder to manufacture on an industrial scale than Tabun, and even by 1945, only a small pilot plant had been set up. By that time, a still more dangerous derivative, pinacolyl methyl-phosphoro-fluoridate had been produced, under the name Soman, though little progress had been made with this by 1945.

It appears that until the factory producing Tabun was overrun by the Red Army in early 1945, the Allies knew nothing of these 'weapons', making their existence one of the best-kept German secrets of World War II. The first the British and Americans knew came from examining shells and bombs recovered from ammunition dumps (about half a million shells and 100,000 bombs, in all), and as the reality of the situation sank in, the researchers were horrified to discover that they were confronted by a lethal agent, and that there was no known cure or antidote from exposure to it. That last factor, it is argued by many, was the real reason that Germany did not employ nerve gas, even in the final days. The Wehrmacht and the SS could not be sure that the enemy did not also possess these simple and cheap weapons of mass destruction, and that the destruction which would result from their use would not be mutually assured.

Index

Page numbers in *italics* refer to picture captions.